MADE MAN (Mafia)

Merka Orion

Contents

1. Chapter 1 — 1
2. Chapter 2 — 8
3. Chapter 3 — 13
4. Chapter 4 — 18
5. Chapter 5 — 22
6. Chapter 6 — 26
7. Chapter 7 — 30
8. Chapter 8 — 34
9. Chapter 9 — 38
10. Chapter 10 — 44
11. Chapter 11 — 48
12. Chapter 12 — 54
13. Chapter 13 — 59

14. Chapter 14 65
15. Chapter 15 70
16. Chapter 16 75
17. Chapter 17 83
18. Chapter 18 90
19. Chapter 19 95
20. Chapter 20 102
21. Chapter 21 110
22. Chapter 22 118
23. Chapter 23 125
24. Chapter 24 134
25. Chapter 25 144

Chapter 1

I heard a gunshot a few blocks away

My face devoid of any emotion

Echoes of a man screaming can be heard from far and wide.

I quietly hid at the back of a nearest thing that I could find but suddenly I heard footsteps walking behind me. My lips are trembling. I closed my eyes while shaking in fear. A man suddenly tapped my shoulder making me flinch. As I opened my eyes I saw a huge dark figure in front of me as I slowly glance my way up to the black shadow.

"Excuse me miss your not allowed here"

I took a deep sigh I thought it was the gun man but it was just the store owner. I said sorry and he left giving me a weird look. I quickly stood up to straighten my shirt. As I felt a strong grip in my mouth making me dizzy and unconscious then everything went to black.

Toot

Toot

Toot

Toot

The loud sound of hanged up telephone wakes her up. She tried to move around only to find her self struggling. She opened her eyes but see nothing just pitch black. There was a black cloth bag over her head and a tape around her hands as well. "Stupid of them just using a flimsy ducktape around my hands". As she move her hands feeling the tightness of the tape covering her wrist.

It's not that tight I think I can easily move my fingers on my left hand.

I slowly cut the tape around my wrist using the ring on my finger. It has a sharp part like a spike that can cut through anything thats not solid. Making the tape hang loose I carefully remove it from my wrist not making any type of sound. Last thing I want is to make a noise and get caught. She tried to breath in and out to calm down her shaky breath. She was tied to a old wooden chair that looks like it could break any second if you touch it. So She stay calmed and slowly take off the black cloth that's over her face. As she opened her eyes. she blink over and over again clearing her foggy vision. Luckily her feet is not taped or anything. As she think of the next step to do.

Escape

I looked around the room scanning every single detail of it. As I saw something that caught my eyes.

Camera, a CCTV

I zoomed my eyes looking straight to the camera and take a good glimpse of it.

There's a red light

Its functioning, that only means it's seeing all the things that Ive done earlier. shit, what should I do. Wait if they already seen everything. then what are they doing? They should be here any second by now. As I heard a noise coming from the other side of the huge metal door. It sounds like two people speaking to each other. I couldn't really make up to what there saying. As I heard a creaking sound coming from the door. I turn my head to that direction looking straight up to the man leaning on the door.

screw it they've already seen everything might as well looked at the person who kidnapped me to analyze his face and observe his body movements.

"Looks like someone is awake" he uttered.

I just stared back, trying to peruse him. Analysing his features and body language. he looks really attractive. He has a messy mint hair, alluring pair of eyes, sharp jawline and a soft looking lips. his body is also quite muscular but his covering all of it. While his arms crossed leaning his body to the door. he looks like he's not impressed of me nor what I did earlier.

After that stare off two boys appear behind him. the first one have a blonde quite rugged hair he looks shorter than the guy beside him. the other man have just a normal dark brown hair he looks quite strong I can tell by the way he display himself. They came in with a rifle on there hands trying to intimidate me. little did they know that I'm not frighten by a gun not even one bit. I've already held a gun not to just touch it but to used it to another human. leaving them breathless on the cold ground.

I'm a part of one of the most notorious and feared mafia organization out there. The Bang. I'm Park So Yeon, 20 years of age. I work for them. they paid me to obtain secret information about hostile, criminals, especially rival gangs. I'm the one who keeps close and secret watch on the actions and words of others. Your a spy and take out enemies to your cause. they assigned me to various espionage missions leaving without any trace and very known for my dexterous and proficient abilities. I also speak multiple languages, which probably helped me get the job. Extreme temperament is needed. They need to know that you won't crack or freak out under potentially extreme pressure. I been through hell and back. Which makes me who I am. but never felt this common emotion called love.

Do I really know who am I working for? well not only i work for them. I have worked with various Gangs and mafia companies to expand my capabilities, intellect and also charm and seduction. not helping that I'm an actress too I can pretend like a victim at this very moment. "Bring her to the room" the mint hair guy said. they just nod at him following everything he ordered like he's the leader. "Yes yoongi" the blonde haired guy said.

So the leaders name is yoongi

"Jimin are you stupid didn't he said he doesn't want to be called by his name after the separation" the black haired guy uttered.

So jimin is the blonde one

"Oh right I have forgotten already" he said. "Shut up you two and bring her to the room" yoongi shouted at the both of them the blonde haired guy gets the black cloth bag on the floor and puts it back over my head for me not to see where there bringing me and the brown haired guy carries me by putting me on his shoulder after he tied my hands back. "Jungkook, She's pretty don't you think" jimin said teasing the young boy beside him. "She's alright" jungkook calmly said not having the reaction jimin wanted. "I could watch her all day if I want too" jimin said with a little bit honesty in his words.

God I already hate both of them

As I heard the door slams opened and me being put on the bed he untied my wrist and takes off the bag over my head.

The door closed

Mission stars now

first i need to take a rest after that cloth they put over my mouth before kidnapping me making me really dizzy and pass out. they put a very strong chemical to it like chloroform. Not only I'm a secret agent I also studied chemical engineering but not the professional one what I mean is the illegal one. I never used a drugs on myself but to the targeted person they assigned me to.

I woke up in the middle of the night I slowly get out of my bed and go towards the door. "of course it's locked" I picked the locks be using the bobby pin in my hair and it opened. "Yes" I carefully opened the door. I make sure to looked around before going out completely. I manage to see where I go despite of the natural darkness that's in my way. There's only one light by the end of the hallway. While walking around I saw four doors. One on my left and two on my right and the room that I came from. I decided to go down stairs.

Finally

While I was walking around the 1st floor were the living room is. I found this weird looking door its made up of mahogany. it's different from the other doors in the house. I wonder whats behind this massive door. As I lean my ears to it. suddenly someone holds my wrist and turned me around forcing me to face him.

"Why are you doing here cutie? It's late at night" jimin said with a husky voice.

"I was trying to find the bathroom" You tried to say as innocent as possible.

"Really? the bathroom is not here though"

shit, what should I do...

Chapter 2

Shit, what should I do...

Pretends to be scared

"Ahh you're hurting me my hands I just wanna go to the bathroom" I whined finally making him let go my hands. "I'm sorry cutie, did I hurt you? my grip wasn't that tight" he said slightly worried I just looked down to my feet. waiting for him to feel sympathy and be force to show me around the house. thinking that he doesn't want me to get lost again. I wait. "Okay fine I'll take you we're the bathroom is and show you around while your here"

Got you

As we're walking through the dark. he turns on one of the light switch and it reveals the massive kitchen with stylish interior. the brass accents balancing old and new. The mix of natural materials used to finish off this kitchen like white marble countertops that makes it stands out.

Kitchen done not that it's important

After the kitchen he walks over to the middle of the house. the living room this might be the place where they stay most of the time and possibly a gathering. It has this elegant traditional design on the window and furniture. Both chairs and the sofa have beautifully rolled arms as well as subtle curves at the back. makes it unique.as I scanned my eyes to the whole room I saw the front door. It looks like it's locked. I snapped to my thoughts when he said something. "Just Incase you didn't notice this whole house is being surveillance with cameras. But I think no ones watching right now."

what would you even tell me that there's no ones guarding it. Stupid, living room done, bathroom next

After I pretends to use the bathroom I asked him if he could also show me around the second floor too just Incase I walked in to the wrong room. he hesitated at first but finally agreed. He's so easy. "I shouldn't be doing this showing you around because your still our hostage and I might get scolded if anyone sees us, but your gonna be here for awhile so why not." "I know, but you're way too nice for your victim. do you even kill people?" I thought Then we head upstairs me following behind him as we reached the last stairs.

he guides me to the dark corridors and pointed his finger to the door to the left. "that's taehyung's room. If you heard weird noises don't panic he's just playing games. I don't know why he needs to be so loud." he stands right in front of the next room just besides taehyung's and said. "this is jungkook's room. if he's not inside he's probably with taehyung playing games." and then he looks over to the room across jungkook's. I followed his gaze. "thats my room right there. if you need anything you can go there and asked me." his finger landed on the door on the right. the last door besides my room. "that's Yoongi's place don't knock if it's not important. he's really grumpy and can get mad easily when you wake up from his sleep. don't test it. Your not gonna be lucky. Okay I warned you. even me and the boys can't touch that door."

Noted, but it feels exciting should I?

"And also I forgot to tell you that you need to knock three times if you need something and four times if your in danger" I just nodded and trails him from behind. I swiftly examine the place before he escort me back to my room but something caught my eyes. Its the picture frame alongside Yoongi's room. It's faintly sideways. It's not noticeable but not for me. I think there's hidden door in this floor. I definitely need to inspect that room. I walked over there with a slow pace. I was about to be in contact with the picture frame. somebody shouted from behind making me stop my tracks and glance back. As I saw taehyung leaning at the door that supports his slender body staring at us. frowning his eyebrow. Jimin rapidly put me behind him shielding me.

"what are you two doing over here? did yoongi ordered you to show her around?the answer is no. yoongi needs to know about this I'm sorry jimin." Taehyung said "But I just showed her around the hallway. there's nothing here anyway" jimin said "Rules is rules and you should know that. you already know what to do go ahead."

snitching ass taehyung

Jimin walked approaching Yoongi's room and taehyung just left me there standing. I decided to eves dropped by the door. I heard loud angry voice it's from yoongi

Jimin tell me what happened!

I showed her around the house...

she's still our hostage!

But she's living here now...

It doesn't fucking matter!

Get out I said get out!

I stand up when I heard footsteps walking closer to the door and immediately run inside my room locking the door. I tiredly walked over my bed and laid my body to the soft cushion and closed my eyes.

Chapter 3

As I woke up from my unpleasant sleep. last night went horribly. from jimin finding me downstairs and actually showed me around and taehyung snitching his own member jimin what a betrayer. and jimin getting harsh words from their leader. I came back to reality when someone knocks at the door making me flinch.

Knock knock

"Are you awake? can i opened the door?" He said. "I'm awake!" I said and he unlocked the door and got inside. he puts this pile of clothing on the top of the dresser beside the door while placing it gently. "this is your clothes for the day don't mess it up or do anything because it's mine." Jungkook uttered and I just nod my head. after that he approached me and sat at the corner of the bed and said. "go ahead and shower after getting ready go downstairs for breakfast Okay, don't waste any time." I stared at him utter in silence not knowing how to respond to his commanding voice. "Or do want me to join you in the shower?" His maddening face changes into a teasing one. "No, thank you." I stand up and hurriedly head towards the bathroom.

I quickly locked the door behind me and look at the pile of clothes that he recently gave me. It's a oversized white shirt big enough to cover above my knees. and a pair of jean shorts. I rest it on the white marble counter near the sink. I stripped my self down and lay the previous clothing that I'm wearing on top of the counter and fold it nicely. as I stepped inside my feet touching the cold tile floor. turning on the knob. a spray of water hits my bare skin. I instantly remember all the stress that i need to wash of my body. the warm water calming my mind like it always do. I don't know how it but it does. after taking a nice bath. I stepped out of the shower and I glance at my reflection on the foggy mirror and talked to my self. god I look horrible I need to take care of my self more, but that's what a hostage suppose to look like. few more days til I get out of here. just accomplish the mission and not get caught. You can do this So yeon.

I get dressed and get out of the bathroom.when I got out I saw jungkook still sitting at my bed. he looks at me from top to bottom. like his judging me if I justify his wardrobe. like what you see. I thought he smiles and looks back at my eyes. "you look really good in my shirt. It's quite big but it's perfectly fits your body." He looked with a smirk on his face. "Can you stop staring at me. It's freaking me out." I uttered and he just shrug and stands up, heading towards the door but he looked back at me and said. "By the way feel comfortable around me I'm not gonna hurt you but if you try anything like escaping or snooping around thats a whole another story. remember your still our captive and I'm still your kidnapper."

When we arrived at the dining table three of the boys are already sitting in their respected chair the table is massive with a white marble design that matches the chair. it has five chairs one on the left taehyung right next to him is jimin. yoongi is in the middle. jungkook sat on the right signaling me to sit beside him. I slowly sit down. as I felt the tension in the room.

Silence

Yoongi decided to break the silence. what are you waiting for eat up. we have a lot of things to do for the whole day. after he speak everyone started eating. "So yeon I need to talk to you meet me in my room." yoongi uttered and I just nod. "by the way taehyung tie her hands."

Oh I forgot I was a hostage

Taehyung sighed and walks towards the counter and grabbed the rope on top of it. like it's designated to be there just Incase. he walks behind me and whisper something while tying my hands together. "don't worry he's not gonna do anything to you. Just bare with him for a bit." I nod

I hurriedly followed yoongi to his room. he seats in the reclining chair leaning his body back and lay his fingers at his lap. he looks really comfortable. maybe he's not scolding me. I sat in the chair across him. he looks at me and flashed a smile.

"Do you even know why your here? Then let me tell you. We are The Tans it's a newly formed gang in Incase you never heard of it." She looked at me with a bored expression. "I don't care about your supid gang. Get me out of here" he chuckled "you shouldn't be sticking your nose to the Places it doesn't belong and a pretty girl alone walking late at night. It's looks like your asking for it. did your parents told you about that?" he's looking at me with a sly smirk on his face. "It's not my fault that I have no parents." I said to him with no sign of emotion "Too bad, but do you remember the man that blew your hiding spot princess?"

The store owner

"What about him? what happened to him?" I said while looking at him worried "He's gone, he's dead, I killed him because he's a witness just like you. but why are you alive? since my eyes met you they've never cared to see anyone else in front of them. because your different. I don't know what it is. all I know is you are special."

"You killed him, you killed the store owner he didn't even do anything to you. you're insane go away from me."

"Are you serious I just admit how I felt about you. but you're still caring about that dead man."

go back to your room!

Chapter 4

His angry voice always making me flinch. he's definitely scarier than namjoon. Namjoon is my boss the one who commands me my special mission. He's also joined with hoseok and seokjin as his right hand. we're all working at the same gang.

I quickly stand up and head towards the door. but before I could open the door someone already opened it. I walked past Jungkook but be held my arms really tight and whisper something. "what is said in the room stays in the room. not even our members knows about this only yoongi me and now you understand." he tightens the grip even more."y-yes now let go of me it hurts." He let go and I run towards my room and bumps to someone. I didn't care to look and enclosed the door. still panting I plop my body to the massive bed and looked at the celling.

While I was walking towards taehyung's room. I saw So yeon comes out of Yoongi's room running and bumped in to me. I looked at the door she just closed and looks at jungkook standing over there. We made eye contact for a second and he left. I continue what I'm doing and heads towards taehyung's room.

"hey taehyung wanna talk?" jimin asked him nicely he's doing this out of boredom. "are you blind? did you see than I'm playing". Taehyung said ignoring him completely. "It's important it's about her and yoongi." he quickly throws the controller and giving jimin his undivided attention while looking at him anticipating on what's he has to say to the couple people he mentioned earlier. "Cmon tell me what's about them?" he's looking at him frowning his eye brows. "looks like someone likes our So yeon I heard them talking when i was behind Yoongi's room. I'm not only mad at that he already broke the agreement we did before the separation. he killed someone and that's why she here. she's a witness of the termination and don't tell anyone I told you this."

"Aish this hyung" Taehyung said in frustration. "Not only yoongi lied about her. He also break his promise to us. after all of this I don't think I can believe him anymore"

"What do you mean by promise?" Jungkook said while approaching his two member and joined them on their boys talk. he also sits on the floor folding his legs and looked at his members. "Did you heard about it? about that liar our suppose to be leader." Taehyung proudly means those words not caring if it's harming anyone. "No and who told you this information?" Jungkook pretended to be oblivious of the situation he's already a part of. "It doesn't matter now what we need to do is talk to him." he said while standing up and signaled them to come with him.

The door slams open

The three boys sit across yoongi and they also called her to join this conversation as well. when she entered the room she immediately sat beside taehyung. While jungkook and jimin is on the other side of the office. "what do you want to talk about?" Yoongi asked the members who harshly barged in his room without his permission. "What happened to our agreement? I remember it says their no lie, no love, no kill." jimin said with a serious tone not forgetting how his facial expression suddenly changes when his mad. He looks scary I've never seen him like this. I like the stupid and caring jimin not like this. but what agreement are they talking about? I was bring back to reality when I heard my name.

"It's So yeon this is all her fault." jungkook said as I felt all their eyes at me. You frown your eye brows not being able to have a say in this conversation. "Jimin who told you this?" Yoongi completely ignoring jungkooks statement as he interrogated jimin the one who bring up the conundrum at the first place. "It doesn't matter what matters is this problem in front of us." jimin abruptly said.

"Then how are we gonna fix this predicament. first step is who told you this. and then we can move on." Yoongi said while looking at the people in front of him right in the eyes. The tension is building up once again until jungkook speaks. "like I already told you it's her, I'm pretty sure she's told them to make us fight as a distraction so she can escape."

That's actually really smart I didn't think of that but I don't want you to get mad and start hating me. I want to all to my side. I will do anything to make that happen.

Even if I need to seduce one of you...

Chapter 5

As I watched yoongi in front of me search my gaze with his eyes almost as if he trying to find something. "Are you the one who told them? Answer me" he scream at me. "How can I even do that. They locked me in my room all day and taehyung didn't you bring me here." I said glaring at him "how can I believe you when yesterday night jimin caught you down stairs. I remember telling jungkook to make sure it's locked" he's looking at me intensely "Well one of your member didn't locked the door, that's how I get out"

Yoongi immediately locks eyes with jungkook sending daggers. jungkook looks away doesn't even protest and left. Yoongi sighed and turn his attention to me. "He's right your trying to break us apart, your gonna get your own consequences no food for a few days just water and you can't get out of that room without any of us escorting you." I looked at him with widen eyes "Are you trying to kill me by starving me? I didn't even do anything" you complained at your rights as a human being. "it's me I spread the information don't punish her it's all my fault" jimin uttered "Tae-hyung bring her back to her room her punishment is dismissed" Taehyung gently guide me outside the room.

"Hey are you okay? I'm sorry about yoongi He's just always like that. Do want me to help you get the stress out of your body" My eyes widen at his statement. "Yah not like that. What I mean is do you wanna play games with me, it's gonna be fun" Before I could say anything he grabs my hand and we both run inside his room. His room is quite large really messy but organized at the same time. It's full of games is not meant just for the kids. With pool, computer, darts and more, there are plenty of activities to keep all ages entertained. His bed is in the corner because of all of this stuff.

"Sit beside me so we can start this game already I've been wanting to play this with someone but non of my hyungs even jungkook wanted to" he sadly said to me This is my opportunity to get tae-hyung at my side. just pretend like your innocent and oblivious. Little does he know I'm the best player out there. not that I'm a gamer but I like guns a lot so this is gonna be easy. I thought "But I don't know how this works?" Pointing my finger at the controller that taehyung's holding. "Let me teach you it works like this the Y button is used to change weapons and The circle and X represent 'yes' or 'no' for decision-making. While putting his hands around me gently wrapping his long arms almost hugging me from the back and guiding me his hands that's rested on top of mines.

After awhile of teaching and pretending. It's finally time for him to see how good this girl can be. Fine I will play your games and you will play mine.

"Not bad for your first time" he said jokingly. "What are you talking about. You lose on a first timer just admit it." I proudly said pretending not to know anything about this games. He's looking intensely at me like he wants a rematch to happened right now or is that what I think it is. "I already like you" A smirk lightly creeps up my lips.

Taehyung done

I still need to have a talk with yoongi without making the beast mad. I just need to get out of here but how? until I heard the door being opened revealing yoongi leaning at the door frame.

Perfect now that your here

"May I talk to you princess? If I'm not bothering you and your new friend" I quickly stand up straighten my shirt and wave taehyung goodbye. I trails behind him entering his room. As I sit beside him. "I thought your gonna need a lot of convincing, but I guess I'm wrong" I forgot about that I'm playing hard to get. "Well I need to get out of there anyways"He smiled flashing me his gummy smile. "I know taehyung can be annoying" I chucked at his statement and asked "Why did I came here for? Are you gonna tell me something? anything important? he lays his hands on top of mine resting it.

"just stay with us and don't plan to escape because I will find you and bring you back. I need you, If I have to explain you wouldn't understand"

Do you hear what your saying yoongi? I looked down and put a piece of hair behind my ear that's in my face and pretends to be flattered and blushed. Perfect I'm gonna use this to my advantage.

Yoongi done jungkook your next.

Chapter 6

I walked out of Yoongi's room and gently closed the door behind me. As a victorious smile rested on my face. I looked around the corridors and notice one door is not completely shut. I walked my way over their and peer at the small gap as I saw jungkook without a shirt on. Perhaps he just get out of the shower. Hair still wet, Water droplets dripping down his back. Trailing every single part of his muscle. He looks godly. As I heard my self gasp and swiftly cover my mouth. But it's too late he already noticed me standing at the back of the black wooden door. He walks over me and pushed me inside his room..

"Why are you peaking at my room? Do you really wanna see this that bad. his finger pointing down to his built abs. As I take a good glance of his beautifuly structured abs. he swiftly pulled my chin up forcing me to look at him. "Too distracted huh" I rolled my eyes and gently push away his fingers on my me. Giving him a seductive smile while I lightly pushed his hard chest making him fall into his bed and held his balance using his elbow looking at me like he's challenging me.

It's my turn to tease you jungkook

I walked my way near him but not enough for him to reach me. I slowly bend my self down enough for him to get a glimpse of my chest but before he could I briskly put my shirt up covering it. I saw a disappointment in his eyes for a second and back at the smirking one. As I unhurriedly picked the black clothing laying on the tiled floor and position my self back up. I throw the black shirt on his face making his stupid smirk fade away. He glares at me. It means He's mad. Wrong move and he's gonna eat me like literally.

He stands up and bit his lip looking up and down at me. If he was ready to devour me. He suddenly grabbed a hold of my waist. Making me jump from his touch. I hold onto his arms in attempt to pull it off of me but his already holding onto me tightly.

I'm stuck, Plan b show him my skills but I don't wanna blew my cover so damn early if I beat his ass right now. Should I shout like what victims do? but that will make it seems that he's trying to touch me. No I need him to trust me not despise me. What should I do? I was pulled back to reality when someone opened the door making jungkook to complete loose his grip around my waist. I stumble a bit but balanced my self back. As I saw jimin looking furious staring right at jungkook. I glance at him. He looked good, like sin in a suit, When his mad. I really need to shrug off this thoughts before I drowned to his striking eyes. not even a second passed I was out of the room. jimin already dragging me somewhere.

"Yah! Jimin it hurts where are you bringing me?" I begged at him. He looked like he didn't even hear me. I sighed and just gave in. Thank your self because if your not jimin. You will be laying in the hard floor groaning in pain in a second. Why did I even accept this mission I asked myself.

It's for my brother

I snapped out in my thought finding my self in front of his room. As jimin called my name I followed his voice. And he's already inside. I walked my way over there and sat at the corner of the bed beside him. And jimin said something.

"Are you okay did he hurt you" he's glancing around my body looking for a bruise or a small scratch. I stoped him and makes him bring his attention back to me. "I'm perfectly fine okay jungkook would not hurt me he's just quite strong" giving him a reassuring smile and he sighed. "Exactly be careful around him.

Luckily he didn't give you a scratch or else" he shook his head and suddenly pulled me into a hug me. I was taken aback at first but return it back.

Looks like I don't have to pursue him.

Chapter 7

As I broke the hug. I gently tapped his shoulder giving him my famous smile.I stood up and walked my way to my room. I glance back at him one last time.He was looking down to his hands fidgeting it. He has this small smile rested on his face. I guess is blushing. I chucked and left.

I laid my body at the massive bed making my body look really small. I took a deep breath and closed my tired eyes as l reminisce all the memories in the past. I miss my family, mom, dad and my big brother. He looks like the same age with some of the boys in house. Maybe a little bit older that jimin. As I felt my self drift to sleep.

"So yeon were are you little girl" I heard a man speak my name in a scary tone making me hid under the bed even further.As I felt my self trembling and scared stiff. I quickly covered my mouth to refrain any sound from coming out. I heard a foots step getting closer and closer. My eyes widen and I heard myself gasp when I saw the mans feet in front of me. he chucked and crouch down enough for him to see my dress that is slightly out for him to notice. He roughly grab my arms and pulled me under the bed making me whine in pain as a newly scratch is made. "Do you know that your really bad at hiding seek. Little girl, stand up your parents wants to see you before they run out of breath." He laughingly said.

As I saw a man and a woman both lying together on the cold ground. His body is lifelessly resting while his before white shirt is soaked with a red color and a pool of red liquid around his body. He looks at me with that weary eyes and manage to speak with unstable breathing. "My little sunshine So yeon-ah f-forgive me and your m-mom for leaving you so e-early. We love you so much""Dad what you saying your not leaving me you can't what about me" I cried out But before he runs out of breath he said something. "Find your brother he's still alive" I felt his hand getting cold by the second.

So yeon...

Wait so yeon...

As I felt a cold hands in my face cupping the side of my cheeks lightly. As I opened my eyes and I saw yoongi on top of me looking very worried. "Hey are you alright, your screaming. So I came here as fast as I can. I heard you say d...dad and something about a b...brother." Before I could speak I saw the door slams o pen."What happened is she okay" jimin said "She's fine now don't worry about it."Jimin placed the tray of food at the nightstand beside my bed and said."Do you want me to feed you? Your still weak from your previous night mare I'm taking care of you for today" I sigh

How the hell am I gonna get out of this room if he's gonna watch me all night. I still need to check out the hidden door from the other day. I need to relax and show him that not exhausted. I still can't believe that I've dreamt about my parents passing again. it's been a month since the last time that happened why is it coming back now. Maybe because I still haven't found my brother. Dad and mom just wait okay. Your suffering is gonna end I'm gonna find who end your life and after this I'm gonna be able see my brother. Namjoon promised me he will find him. That's why I'm here doing this mission. And risking my life it's for them. my family.

"Jimin I'm fine you can leave I can eat by my self I'm not a child okay, I've been living independently for my whole life. I don't need your pity" jimin eyes widen"When did I say I'm doing this for pity. So yeon i wanna take of you because I want to no ones forcing me or ordering me to do this" he said while he holds my hands."I'm sorry jiminie I didn't mean t-" she was cut off when jimin suddenly hugged her really tight not letting go any second."Jimin you're heavy please let go" she complained. Jimin broke the hug and looked at her one last time before leaving.

What was that? He's acting weird lately

Id feel like I need to follow him and say my apologies. As I head towards the door. I heard them running in the corridors. And when I opened the door. All of them were gone. It looks like their having a meeting in Yoongi's room. I walk my way their and lean my ears towards the door. Quietly listening to what their saying. I heard this angry voice which is very familiar. It's yoongi he says. "Jungkook found a teenage boy lurking around the house.""But our location is very hidden" jimin uttered. "I know that's why we need to be careful going in and out of the house" jungkook spat. "Then who do you think it is?" Taehyung said. "He's probably a spy from the other gang trying to get information" yoongi ended the conversation.

Perhaps our worst enemy The Bang...

Chapter 8

My eyes grew wider when I heard the name of the company that I'm working for that I'm currently on a mission. I heard footsteps getting closer to the door. And the sound of the knob turning. I immediately snicker away from there and head back to my room. I breath in and out and sat on my bed.

I wait for the sun to go down and started planning my next step. I need to see what their hiding behind that wall. I slowly opened the door without it creaking and scan the whole floor I didn't see anything. All their doors are closed. I think their already asleep. I smoothly crouched over their at the end of the hallway. Without the cameras getting a glimpse of me. Only one camera in the second floor.I position my self back up and sprayed water at the CCTV. Making it blurry only for a few minutes. I need to be fast. I swiftly turned the picture frame from side to side touching every single corner of it. Until it finally opened. Making a little bit of noise.

I need to hurry. I only have four minutes til the water dried down. The brick wall started opening creating a small gap.

I fit my petite body on the small passage the door only gave me. I slowly closed it and turn my back away from the hidden door. I closed my eyes. From the bright light. One by one the light opens up.I wasn't shocked by the view in front of my very eyes. The walls are full of weapons hanged up. They have all sorts of guns like rifle, shotgun and sniper rifle. Also all kinds of knives and hand grenade. But my eyes is looking for something else. And then it landed on a metal box shaped in the middle of the room. it looks like a safe.As a smile creeps up my lips. I hurriedly go over there and opened the box. "Of course is has a freaking code." As I remember taehyung and jungkook talking earlier.

"Taehyungie did you already change the code that hyung assigned you?" Jungkook whispered

"Yes i did. so I can easily remember when we're in a hurry. It also means the four of us" Taehyung proudly said

"Are you serous that's so easy anyone would guess that"

"What do you want me to do? It's already donePlus how can even anyone could figure how to get in that room. It's impossible"

"Okay just shut up taehyung someone might hear us"

There so loud that I can hear it upstairs. And thank you for the information idiots.

It also means the four of us? As I touch the buttons with numbers that I have in mind. And it unexpectedly opens up. How stupid can they be 0444 really taehyung? The metal door finally opened. exposing a ton of money and piles of drugs. That's it no files or folders. I guess it's negative. Maybe they have another hideout. I need to find where that is.

I was about to get out but my eyes caught something. I gaze up to the walls of guns. "I don't think they would mind if I borrow one of their guns" I swiftly hide in under my shirt and get out of that place.

I gently put the gun under my pillow. Making it sure it's locked and safe. I rest my head on the pillow and pull the silky sheets over my head. And drifted to dreamland.

I was woken up by the banging on my door. I think that's jungkook he still hates me from what happened yesterday. I'm not blaming him. It's his fault that his skipping bases. As I pulled my self out of bed and opened the door. Looking at him with a bored expression on my face."Hurry up and get ready we're leaving in an hour" he throws the clothes in my hands. "Where are we going?" I asked

"I can't tell you not now. you're gonna know when we arrive their."

Chapter 9

You exited your room and move your way downs stairs making your steps as light as possible. When you reached the last step. You walked your way over their. As you neared the kitchen you heard the voices of the boys. Their talking about something. You tried to make up to what their saying. And hide yourself behind the wall and listen carefully.

"We need to.....our location....before...Come...show up....we don't want that"

"Where is she....done...get her....and put a burlap sack....face....g et ready..."

You remove yourself away from the wall. As you stepped your feet inside the kitchen. The voices inside the room take a brief pause but soon enough they became loud again. Taehyung started greeting you while jungkook staring right at you. yoongi and jimin signaled you to sit by them in huge table. You sat beside jungkook who rudely woke you from your beautiful sleep. Jimin and Taehyung's face begun to pout. Because you sat with jungkook and not them. "Eat up and then we leave" Including yoongi but he doesn't really show it.

You feel your body bounce by the second.Like it's following the flow of the car making its way in to a bumpy road. it sounds like we're inside the woods or a forest. You can't see anything it's just darkness. Because earlier before you leave jungkook put a black bag over your head for you not to see where your heading. As you felt a presence near you You slightly move away but then he hold your arms and guide you gently outside.Your vision lighten by the bright light in front of you. Not quite enough for you to see where you're going. As you heard the door closed someone had already taken off the black cloth over your head. You squint your eyes adjusting from the light. You immediately open them and looked around the room in front of you.

"What is this? Abandoned house?" It looks quite scary like it's from a horror film. Broken cabinets, century old sofa, shuttered window and a bedroom. But Somethings not quite right. Then you remember last night the hidden passage which has walls of guns and a stash of money and not forgetting about the gun that you stole. Which you securely hid under your shirt this morning

Before you leave and the sideways picture frame. It means there something more than a old broken cabinets in this place.Speaking of broken cabinets it looks like this one is perfectly placed in here. I slowly looked around for any sign of the boys. Nothing. I quickly roam my hands touching all the knobs and things on top of it. Until I accidentally drop one of the books but before it could touch the floor. I swiftly gabbed it before it fall and make a loud sound. Last thing I want is to get caught.

As I looked back up my eyes grew wider when the cabinet unexpectedly opened Revealing a much larger space fancier than the previous one. It has a big chandelier with beautiful white lights hanging underneath the living room. But Before you can fully enter. That was then you heard somebody clear their throat behind you. You bolted around and you were facing Jungkook. Your face we're just a couple centimeters away from one another. He's staring deeply into your soul. But he stoped when he heard jimin's voice and some people had already come in.

"Jungkook how did you opened that so quickly" jimin curiously asked.

"Well it's not me who opened it. ask the girl right here" making them glance at me.

"I accidentally bump to cabinet when I was wondering around and suddenly a book fell out" I hesitantly said.

"Oh well then we don't have to tell you. You already figure it up your self"Taehyung said and he runs up to me holding my hands and pull me inside.

I still can feel jungkook staring at me from the back. It feels like it can get through my skin. Jimin also trails behind us. He's a little far because of his short limbs. Trying to catch up with me and taehyung.

You felt your self sinking in the plushy bed.Definitely softer than the last one. Your head is gently resting on the velvety pillows. while your eyes is stuck staring at the ceiling. As you remember what happen earlier.While your walking with taehyung around the house. You vaguely scan the hallways your passing by. The a door at the end of the hallway it looks the same as the mahogany door from the last house. Maybe that's the office where yoongi always held the meeting with the boys.And beside the office. I saw this door theirs something written on it. I think it starts with the letter T and ends with G.Wait Is it a Training room. After that thought my mind wondered like why would they label it knowing that they have a hostage running around the house. they're really comfortable with me. I wonder if namjoon already knows where they bring me. I was pulled backed to reality when. I heard someone knocked on my door.

Suddenly Jimin opened the door looking a bit frustrated. I glanced at him trying to read his expression but I couldn't read it."what's wrong jimin are you alright" I touched his face slightly cupping the side of his cheek. He was tense at first but soften after. He looks cute while resting his face at my hands. I smiled to my self.

"I'm sorry let's go" he turns around but before he can I already got a glimpse of his angelic smile. I don't know why but it makes my heart flutters. I stop my thoughts when he grabs my hands and run somewhere. Before I could speak the door was opened. It's Yoongi's office.

"Now that your here I'm going straight to the point. Did you steal the gun?"

As I felt my body tensed up. feeling the gun against my waist where I placed it earlier. But didn't let them notice. I put my straight face on and picked my words carefully.

"No, how can I even know where your things are. Maybe you have misplaced it" I confidently answered.

"Well what about earlier jungkook told me that you figure out how to opened the suppose to be secret passage" yoongi uttered

"As I said it was accidental" I said looking straight at Yoongi's eyes. Telling him by my gaze that I'm not lying.

"Let's not go any further. If theirs no point." But jungkook insisted and said.

"So my gun disappeared just like that" he shook his head and left stomping his feet.

So that's he's gun that's why he's so furious.

He heard his name being called from a distance but he decided to ignore it and go to his room. The man that called him just sighed and gave up.

So Yoongi trust me better than his own.

Chapter 10

You felt a quick tap on your shoulder. You decided to ignored it. You felt another tap but this time it was a little hard. It looks like it's not going away on its own. You turn around and looked at the person with a bored expression. It was jimin looking at me like wants to say something. As I watched him deeply sigh and scratch at the back of his neck. Now I'm curious of whats inside of that little mind of his. I decided to ask him.

"Jimin you wanna talk about something?"

He looked at me like he wants me to follow him so I did. As I closed the door behind me. We sat at his bed simultaneously. I waited for the atmosphere to become awkward for him to start speaking. I smiled at him while I rest my hands on top of his. Making him comfortable in an instant.

"Earlier me and jungkook fought about you."

Making me put all of my attention to him.

"He really thinks that's you steal the gun and I told him that it's impossible for you to even get hold of that. Plus I know that your scared of it and wouldn't even dared to touch it"

I nod at his statement.

"But now his mad at me. I can't go a day without fixing our fight for some stupid reasons. I owe him a lot since day one and I don't want this to be the end of our friendship"

I nod as a signal for him to continue.

I few years ago when I was walking at night. suddenly a herd of man surrounded me and start beating me to pulp. There are the one who killed my mother because she didn't pay them. And don't have the money for it. We hide until they finally found us and shot her. I was lucky to got away but my mother wasn't.They go all the way to find me. By taking my life as a replacement for my mother's debt. I can't go to the police because they have connection. I don't know what to do. Not until I met jungkook he was young at that time and we make a strong bond then and there. And led me to this gang as a home. but he tells me the only way is to punish them the other way around. If they take life then life will be taken out of them. But I regretted it as quick as it occurred. I can't kill I don't want to. I'm worried about you I don't want us to have the same ending. But Were both stuck here. there's no turning back now.

Not realizing a tear got out of my now watery eyes and the rest stream down my face. I quickly covered my face and wipe the tears. But before I could he kissed my tears away. I felt his soft lips against my pink dusted cheeks. I just closed my eyes wanting the sensation to linger. But Suddenly he moves his lips away from my cheeks and it landed on mine. It was soft and tender at first. As he kiss the top of my lips, the bottom of my lips. making it long as it last. We just gaze at each other for awhile.

Not knowing that someone's eyes are peering at them. it was Jungkook.

Meanwhile a huge smile creeps to his lips as he's gaze at the bright screen in front of his very eyes. "I know where they are"The mans said while he leans his back at the chair and put his hands to touch his chin.

"Namjoon when do you wanna head their" as the man with red hair said while leaning his body to the door frame.

"few more days. I just need to be certain about some things" As the man in desk uttered.

"What more do you need I'm sure that's it." As the blonde guy said while shoving a piece of fruit to his mouth.

"But how do you know that's the exact location" the red haired guy asked.

"Before we put her in this mission. I place a tracker device at the back of her neck, I don't even know if she notice it herself, all I know is this is the area that she led us to is precise"

"And how do know she's doing her job right?"The blonde guy hair uttered.

"She can be rebel at times but this mission is no joke. She's risking her life not for us nor for the gang but for her brother and if she failed...

Then she will never see her brother alive...

Chapter 11

You waited a minute before walking out of Jimin's room. And rested your whole body in the door behind you. Breathing in and out. You took a moment to gather yourself, And then stepped forward. But before you could someone grab a hold of your wrist. He was mad, real mad and you know how short tempered he is. When it comes to you. Though you have no idea why is he mad at the first place. So you just let him dragged you to wherever. You just don't want him to be mad than he already is.

He slams his door closed and stared at you for a while. I could feel his eyes peering through me. His gaze became darker and darker by the second. And me still clueless of what's the reason he's acting like a beast trying to eat me up alive.

Cmon So yeon what are you doing your not afraid of him.

You glare back at him. Trying to intimidate him. As You step your self forward making him step back. As I get closer and closer. Until one of his feet hits the bed. But before he falls back I held him by his shirt making him bring back his balance.

"What's wrong with you jungkook?" I said while crossing my arms with frowned eye brows. "No what's wrong with you? I saw you and jimin. Yes I saw everything."

"What are you trying to implie"

"You know that if yoongi caught you together with jimin he will get furious and make your situation worst than it already is not only you but also Jimin's"

Don't let your heart act for you

"I heard it. Fine, what do you want me to do?"

"I want you to kiss me just like what you did earlier with him and yoongi will not know anything about you and jimin"

What a pervert boy he is

"What are you waiting for? or you want yoongi to know about you and jimi-"

She cut my words and in just a second I'm already at my bed. She pushed me and crawl in to my lap and sits comfortably on top of my thighs. She leans her face closer to mine until our nose touches. We're both breathing in sync like our heart beat is beating in sync. She brushed her lips with mine lightly touching it. I just wanna feel her glossy lips against mine already. She loves to tease me so much. She has no idea that's it's making me like her even more.

But before our lips touch. You rest one of her finger on his soft lips stopping him from kissing me but it makes him even want more. He suddenly opened his eyes and gaze at me. You gaze him back and gave him a seductive smirk.

Patience

But before he could protest the door flew opened. Revealing jimin standing in the door. I quickly remove myself from jungkook and run to jimin putting my arms around him and pretends to sob. As he glance down at me and return the hug.

"Jungkook what are you trying to do with her don't you dare come near her again."

"But hyung she's the one who's trying to do something with me."

"Do you think I would believe you, your clearly the man here and your ten times stronger than her"

"But Hyung I need to explai-"

"Save it, i don't wanna hear about it, you can defend yourself when I'm not furious at you"

He pulled me outside his room. Leaving jungkook confuse and frustrated. Not because he didn't get to kiss her but now jimin will think that he threaten her to come with him inside his room.

He held my shoulder tight and gaze at me softly. "Did he touch you anywhere? Tell me so I could tell yoongi and he will sure get his consequences"

"No please don't tell yoongi about what happen I might get my punishment too."

He sigh deeply and wraps his arms around you and gladly hugged him back. Not realizing a smile creeps up to your face and back to the sad one when he broke the hug.

"Okay I will not tell yoongi not because of him but because I don't want you to get hurt"

He hugged me once again and whisper something to my ear. "But if I see you around jungkook again I will be mad and you don't wanna see that understand." He softly gaze down at you.

"Yes jiminie" he chuckled at my cuteness.

We stop our tracks when we heard a voice coming from the door behind us. Sounds like taehyung and yoongi. Then the door slams opened revealing taehyung. He looked quite mad. I wonder what it is.

"Where have you been Yoongi's been trying finding you. He wants to talk to the both of you now" You felt yourself stiffen by the Stares Yoongi's giving you. But then he stop when someone enters the room.

"Now that jungkook is here let's start. We found another spy walking around our area we confront him in a nice way to whom gang is he belong but we get nothing so we decided to capture him and put him in the basement. He's gonna be there until he said something."

"If not what do we do? Do we kill him?"

After Jungkook said all eyes are on him. But then he chuckled and so our the boys. Like what is wrong with them I'm surprise I haven't died in their hands. As I watched them talking and then it became silence again. Yoongi's gaze is back to me. I know what he wants. He wants to talk to me but without the other boys around just us. He dismissed the meeting. all of them left excluding me. Now I'm left with the monster Min Yoongi.

"If you think that I already forget what you did the other day your wrong. I'm watching your every little move"

"So you don't believe anything that I said. Do I have to do you a favor or something"

He chuckled at my last statement. He stand up and leans his face closer to my neck and whisper something. I can feel his warm breath tickling my ears. Making my body suddenly tense up.

"No you don't have to princess, now that you've heard everything. We're not gonna let you go anymore. Your gonna stay here with me, with us. Just don't try to do stupid things like escaping you hear me"

He moves his face away from mine and give me his mischievous smile. That's sends shivers throughout my whole body.

Chapter 12

Night fell without realizing that you've been in your bed thinking about the four man living with you in this house. You can't seem to sleep. Maybe because of what happen between you and jungkook. You can't take him off of your mind. You're the one who's suppose to make him think about you night and day not vice versa.Which makes you frustrated. You don't really know the reason why and you're not planning to know sooner or later.

So yeon-ah

So yeon wake up

Just give me a Minute

You little sunshine did you already forget?

What is it dad

Just wake up and I'll tell you

I dont want too its still early

So yeon...

Wait that doesn't sound like dad. And what is he wanna tell me. You felt a gentle tap on your arms. That makes you opened your eyes and realize it was only a dream. You looked at the person who woke you up and gaze at him briefly. You rubbed your eyes before getting out of bed.

"Where are you going? You're not thanking me for waking you up from your previous nightmare"

"It's not a nightmare you idiot, and I'm going to the bathroom, you can leave now taehyung"

"Okay but after breakfast can we play again? I wanna spent time with you today"

"Fine whatever and don't wait for me after I came out of the bathroom"

"Whatever you say" he chuckled and left.

After another hour of awkward breakfast.The food they serve us is made up of thick blocks of tension and a weird atmosphere. we slowly evaporate from the dinning table and go to our own respective rooms. Until now I can still feel the tension between me and jungkook. We haven't talked since that day. Not helping that yoongi is glancing at me once in a while and pretends to eat his food. And jimin being uncomfortable around his best friend jungkook. Taehyung is the only normal one now which is rare. I can sense it even thought their good at hiding it. I need to get out of this mess and focus on my new target taehyung. He's already comfortable around me but I need more than that. I want his trust and loyalty. I need to dug deep to get all the dirt he's been hiding.

As you leaned your body to the door. He immediately notice your presence and signal you to sit next to him. By tapping the sit beside him. You excitedly sat on the marble floor and gaze at him with a smile on your face.

"I haven't been around with a girl like you in a long time" I gulped at his statement.

"What do you meant by that?"

"That's why I'm so excited when yoongi hyung brought you here. You reminded me of my little sister too bad she left this world already"

I glanced at him worried and held his hand lightly squeezing it. Waiting him to get comfortable. And he finally opened up.

One day I was walking happy with her and then very loud noise can be heard from the street across us. It's sounds like gunshots. Somebody is showering the town with bullets. I quickly hid her behind me and runaway while we're running I saw blood dripping from her back and then she suddenly stopped running and lost her balance and she started breathing slowly. I watch my little sister slowly losing her life in front of my very eyes.which makes me devastated because she's all I have. I don't have anyone besides her. And I don't know what to do I was really young dumb and stupid and the only thing that's in my mind is to get back at them. Then yoongi found me and let me join this insane gang. but then after I get my revenge by taking their life one by one. I started to feel guilt and remorse. All I know is I did this for her and I can't do this ever again. Not for revenge nor for stupids commands.

Taehyung got cut when someone opened the door and call his name. He hurriedly stood up and followed jungkook. Before they could go further I quickly trailed behind them and saw them entered Yoongi's office. I lean my ears to the wooden door and eavesdrop to their conversation. As I heard Yoongi's voice getting mad by the second. You already know some good news is about to spill. Well only for you.

"Our other hideout is destroyed it was bombed and looted they also take all our resources. our weapons, money and drugs and the worst things is they left noting but ashes" he said

"I wonder how they know where exactly our resources located only us four knows about this" jungkook uttered

"Don't forget about her now that she knows everything she can't get out of this house until she die or some miraculous god will save her" he said

"Can't you stop blaming her she's just a victim, she can't be doing all your accusations" jimin abruptly said

"Jimin's right she's too innocent to be doing that and that's impossible, she doesn't even know how to use the controller, if so trying to bomb our house. She's doesn't even know where's that located" taehyung uttered

"You've got a point taehyung" jimin replies

"You have no idea what your talking about" jungkook spat making all of the boys in the room glare at him.

You position yourself back and slowly go towards your room. As you pressed your back at the door. You heard the door open and close from the other side. It means they left Yoongi's office.

Few more days and I'll be out of this hell.

Chapter 13

As the man in all black with red hair entered the room. He sat in the couch making himself comfortable. While the other man with blonde hair sits across him. The man in the black desk moves his hand. Signaling them so speak. And then puts his hands back clasping it together.

"Hoseok have you done the mission I assigned you to?"

"Yes Namjoon, The placed is completely destroyed. Nothing left but ashes"

"Good, how about you mister seokjin?"

"Yes Namjoon, I have found the location exactly where she told us and collected everything and anything I could find.The resources are being transferred to our safe house. And what do want me to do with it"

"Just keep it tacked and safe they may need that soon" namjoon uttered

"But why do I feel bad for her, knowing she's not getting anything back after this successful mission that she helped us with"

"Were not certain yet. If her mission is successful like we want it to be. Then she will get something from it. But she doesn't need to know that"

They just nod in agreement.

"Prepare yourselves we're coming for you"

As the man in the desk leaned back to his chair resting both of his hands on the arm rest. Planning the next step he has in his broad mind.

You felt yourself getting frustrated by the second. Because your gonna spend another day in hell with them. You always felt yourself burning from their stares and the tension in the dining room. It always gets you. You felt the need of fixing this somehow. As your mind gives you an idea. Why not cooked for them dinner. Maybe they will calmed down when they taste my cooking. You hurriedly gone down stairs luckily no ones there so you so straight to the kitchen and get the Ingredients from the fridge you were shocked it was fully stocked. You bring out the food out and placed them at the wooden cutter and started slicing the fresh vegetables. You heard a noise but you decided to ignore it and continue slicing the other produce. Suddenly you felt a hands snuck into your waist and rest his chin on your shoulder.

"What are you doing here by yourself"

"I want to cook dinner for all of you, and please get off of me. Your distracting me"

"Just making sure your not putting poison in the food your preparing for us"

"Then you can watch me over there, not holding me like this, it's uncomfortable"

"But I wanna say sorry even though it's not my fault. You're the one who's trying to seduce me the other day"

"Jungkook your not even apologizing" he chuckled and slowly pulls his body away from you. And leans his physique body to the counter. Crossed arms with his firm biceps showing through the thigh white shirt his wearing. As he watch you watching you cook.

"Jungkook can you stop looking at me like that it's weird"

"But you're the one here who told me to watch over you and I don't wanna look away from this beautiful view in front of me" I glared at him and he just gave me a smile and come closer towards me. He leans his face closer to mine.

We can only hearing each other's breathing nothing else not even the loud sound of the frying greens. I closed my eyes not knowing what to do. In just second his lips crashed against mine. Our lips moving softly together like it's matching perfectly for each other. Is this what cloud nine feels like. As he broke the kiss. He gaze at me deeply. Forehead still touching. As l glance to his lightly parted lips. But before he could kiss me again. We heard creaking noises coming from the stairs. We pulled away from each other. Me going back to what I'm cooking and him ended up scratching his neck.

"So yeon I've been finding you but you're not in your room. Wait are you cooking dinner for us"

"Taehyung don't worry I'm almost done"

"And you jungkook what are you doing here. Last time I check is you despise her"

"I do, I'm just checking if she's putting poison to our dinner that's why I'm here"

Taehyung seems to agree with jungkook.You just ignored them and continue what your doing. After the we ate the food you prepare they surprisingly like it. All you can hear is only good things from the boys. The only thing is with yoongi he's too quiet while eating his food.But also taehyung tells me that if he's acting like that's then he's really enjoying the food. Your plan go smoothly to make them reunite and break the tension every time we have eat together. But then jimin suddenly wants to talk to you about something he didn't mention what's it's about. So you head to upstairs after you finished cleaning the table. You saw him laying on the bed while his hands is on the top of his head gazing at the ceiling. He quickly sat up when he notice your presence. You sat on his bed right next to him. He gaze at you with his weary eyes. You suddenly started to get worried.

"What happen jimin why do you look so tired?"

"I just got back outside. Yoongi give me a ton of works today. But I manage to go through with it. Because I know when I go home I can finally see you"

"Jimin what are you saying, let's stop this before yoongi and the boys get suspicious"

"So yeon I cant stop this feelings anymore, I like you. Do you like me too? It's fine if you don't" he gaze at me with his glistening eyes.

You started questioning your self who do you really like. Or are you even capable of loving someone. Despite of never having a chance to be in someone's shoulder, caring, worrying and loving you. You never felt that before. That's why this is a new feeling for you. The over flowing of emotions and your heart constantly beating for a specific someone. But you don't know where it belongs. Jimin makes you feel safe and protected when I'm with him. But why does jungkook makes my heart beat like crazy every time his near you. I need to stop these thoughts you don't love someone you can't. Your better than this So yeon.

You can't let your heart act for you.

Chapter 14

You felt yourself rolling around the silky bed feeling tried and frustrated. Maybe Because you have an unpleasant sleep in the fast few weeks. and also you cant help but to think about the two men. That suppose to be your kidnapper but what happens is the other way around. During the few days you've spent here things throughout the house change drastically and not in a good way.

Let's start with the leader he leaves the house frequently and sometimes with jungkook. Probably doing some dealing or scouting for a new hideout. I'm only left with jimin and taehyung most of the time. They've become more strict what I mean is protective around me. I've been in my room for the whole week. The other day he left a tray of food outside my door. and not let me eat with them. And jimin constantly visiting my room asking me if I need something. And It becomes a routine.

But this day is gonna be different. As I grab a hold of my gun that surprisingly they haven't notice and placing it under my big navy blue shirt. Right above my Jean shorts. I walked over to the mirror. As l glance at my reflection. Making sure it's not noticeable for the boys to see. I picked the locks from the door. Because they locked it every time. I looked around the hallways. When I reached the bottom stairs. I heard taehyung and jimin whispering but not just whispering they sound like their hiding from something.

Taehyung text yoongi ASAP

tell them some intruders is lurking around the house

But what if they figured how to get in

Then we escape now with her

Before I could stand up somebody pulled me down making me fall on his chest. I glance at the person and my eyes widen. "Be careful next time babe you might fall again thank god I catch you"

"Shut up hoseok you're the one who pulled me down here, plus I'm not your babe"

"Hey I'm sorry I missed you it's been almost a month without seeing you and it's driving me crazy"

"Don't be loud they might hear us" I whispered.

He's jung hoseok my partner in crime not like a couple though. He's always pair with me in the assigned mission. We've known each other for almost a year now. He's one of my only friends that I trust my life with. He's like an older brother and can be very protective when it's come to me. I used him as an inspiration and motivation when I'm feeling down luckily he's really good at it. But one day He admit his feelings towards me but unfortunately I only see him as a brother. But that didn't changed anything we're still close and comfortable to each other. But If he knows about these boys liking me he might get furious. No one knows what might happened.

Hoseok drag me under the stair case. It's quite dark so even in the daylight it's impossible to see. As I heard taehyung go upstairs. In a few seconds we heard him whisper enough for jimin and us to hear.

She not there

What do you mean?

She's gone

We can't leave without her

We have no choice

It's either her or us

Shit let's go

How dare they leave me just like nothing happened between us through those past months. Their gonna pay for this mark my words you two.

"I'll take care of them for you" hoseok whispered into your ears earning a smirk creeps up to your lips.Taehyung immediately head down stairs but when he reached the bottom step he saw jimin already knocked out and just a few second he felt a sharp pain in his back and everything went black.

□

"Hey stop that it's making me dizzy" Yoongi complained at the young man next to him who keeps throwing his phone at the air then catching it back."I'm sorry it's just I'm worried about them, Do you think she's okay with just the two of them" jungkook worryingly said. "I told them to not be occupied by playing games or other works so they can watch her. Why are you so concerned about her?" His hyung asked him curiously. "I just wanna make sure there okay, nothing else" he replied. "Get ready I think there around the block" jungkook started into thinking.

Why do I feel uneasy at this very moment. I feel uncertain about something. I keep repeating Yoongi's words in my head. Why are you so concerned about her? I notice that lately I can't sleep and all I can think about is her. The feeling of her soft pink lips pressed against mine. Since the day we kissed I can't stop repeating the scene in my head. I feel like jimin is trying to take her away from me. And now that I'm always gone with yoongi. He can spent all time with her. I know that this feeling is wrong. I can't fall in to her web. But I guess I'm trapped around her fingers already. I was pulled out of my thoughts when I heard Yoongi's phone rings.

No ones gonna bother him only if there life is in danger...

Chapter 15

The young man felt his head aches as he's limp body is laying on the cold concrete floor. He tried to open his weary eyes. but he sees nothing filled only with darkness. He heard a man groaning right beside him and he immediately thought that's his friend taehyung he whisper to the laying body beside him. "Taehyung is that you?" The man just groan as a respond. But before he could ask him again the door flew open. He can hear foot steps it sounds like heels. His eye brows frown under the cloth over his eyes. He tried to listen more to their conversation. A voice of a man and a woman can be heard in the whole room.

"What are we gonna do now?" She said

"We just wait for the two to come and proceed to the plan" he uttered

"I think you knocked them out hard, look there's still sleeping" she replied

"That's not even enough, because when they come and witness them in this situation there gonna know were not playing"

As he eavesdrop deeper to the conversation his eyes grew in shock. Because the voice of the woman speaking is oddly familiar. Way to familiar like the more and more he listen his heart sinking deep into the bottom of his stomach. He doesn't wanna believe ears but his mind is already convince of who she was. He was pulled out of his thoughts when the man standing above them speaks he immediately realize who the voice of the man belongs too.

"Take the cloth over their eyes, and put them in the chair there coming" namjoon uttered.

He felt a heavy thing stepping at the side of his weak limbs forcing them to stand up on their own. He lift himself up. While somebody guide them to the chair. He sat and breath heavily feeling his body getting tired by the second. As he felt a soft hand touch his purple bruise making him groan. But the hand softly caress his cheek. the very touch is familiar. Which makes his stiff body softens in a second but back when it occurred. As he remembered the person who did this horrible thing to them. As the woman in front of him leans closer only a few centimeters to his face. He engulfed the strong perfume of the woman its smells like flowers and vanilla. her scent lingering at his nose stills. Which makes him high every time she's this close to him. As he felt a whisper near his neck. her warm breath leaving him a tingling sensation.

"I'm not sorry for what I did or what I will do next but I appreciate the kindness despite of everything that occurred" she whispered.

He respond with a husky voice

"Who are you? And why are you doing this to us? you're not the woman I thought I liked"

"All I want you to do is to forget about meJust pretend that nothing happened"

His heart sunk to the pit of his stomach after hearing the last words that escaped her lips. As he felt his blindfold getting untied and slowly hang loose around his neck. He squint his eyes adjusting from the light above him. His gaze move up and down looking shock of what's he's seeing right in front of him. He seeing a unbelievably beautiful woman with her arms crossed, standing all. wearing this all back tight latex bodysuit. That fits her body perfectly like a glove. showing all of her curves flauntlessly and her long brown hair in a high pony tail lightly resting on her shoulders. She cleared her throat making him look away for staring at her for quite sometime. As he glance over to his side and saw taehyung's jaw dropped. Having the same reaction as him.

"Whoa So yeon my little sister I don't know you can be this hot" taehyung said which makes the people in the room chuckled quietly. Not because it's hilarious but you never heard something like that while in this situation.

"Shut it before I do something to you" she said making him quite shock by the words come out of her mouth. He never thought she will never say something like this.

The door slams opened

Making all the attention at the door. The two man makes their grand entrance. Holding a gun in tied to their hands. Pointing to the opponent around them. Until the tall man speaks. Making them instantly gaze at him.

"Hoseok, seokjin put the gun down we don't need to use violence if we want them to earn trust their back." Namjoon uttered and yoongi chuckled at his announcement.

"What are you talking about namjoon there's no trust to start from in the beginning"

"I know that negotiating would not do anything. That's why we're doing this the hard way. We destroy everything you own even the house your currently living in. But don't worry your resources are safe you can only get it back. if you decided to come back to our gang"

"Bastards" Yoongi curse in his breath

But jungkooks eyes never left her since they came. Staring intensely making her uncomfortable under his sharp gaze.

Chapter 16

As she felt her body slowly getting stab by those deadly stares he's sending her until she cannot anymore. She feels the need to explain everything despite of him not believing what's gonna come out of her lying mouth. She glares back at him trying to talk to him using her orbs. Not until he decided to speak. Breaking the tension inside the four enclosed isolated walls surrounding them.

"What the fuck are you doing here with them? Everything was a setup and planned everything huh? So yeon I'm not asking again" jungkook said full of rage as he peered at her ferociously while she felt ungainly not tolerating his stares anymore. "It's not for you to know what I'm doing here and It's none of your damn business" you sternly said making jungkook groan in sudden frustration while he shook his head vigorously. "I cannot believe this. So are you telling me that everything that happened between us is all lies too" he said the words you've been avoiding to come of of his mouth since they arrived. Your not safe anymore when it comes to him.

"So yeon what's this none sense. what is he talking about did something happen between you two. You know this is not acceptable" Namjoon fumingly said not expecting something pathetic can come out of this. "Let me finish my words namjoon. Nothing happened between us. It's was all part of my job to get close to them and get information"

"Are you fucking kidding me?" Yoongi spat those harsh words not specifically on you but to everyone in this room. "Excuse us" I said while I bow on the boss as a respect and left the tensioned room.

I immediately grabbed jungkooks arms dragging him outside of the room away from your boss and the people inside the area. He roughly removes my grip around his arms and push it away. He stared right at me waiting for me to speak. "Jungkook do you hear what are you saying earlier. There's nothing going on between us"

"So it's true that you didn't feel anything between us. But your action doesn't show the same. Tell me that every time we kissed you didn't feel anything not a single thing for me!" He clenches his jaw while looking at you with his raging facial expressions.

"Jungkook stop this just take your heartbreak and leave, don't you worry about me"

"No I'm tired of hiding this shit. Since the day you entered my life everything change my members they all started falling in love with you and you still have no clue. And then when your kissing me I felt happy that you chose me. Rather than any one of them. That's when I started falling for you. Yoongi already know everything about you and jimin. He saw it too. But didn't say anything because we don't wanna lose you. I've always have this feelings towards you but I kept denying it because it's not allowed but can't anymore."

Before she could protest his lips crashed against her. Pushing her against the wall. She tried to pulled away but doesn't really want to. He grabs her hands and pinned them above her head. At first it was hot and rough full of anger and lust but it became passionate as he soften after. He loosen the grip to her hands. she didn't waste time but to kissed back resting her hands at his chest not realizing there's someone peering at them. She pulled away after a few seconds with a soft gaze in her eyes. They breathe in sync trying to catch a breath after that heated locking of lips they weren't expecting to happen, Until he speaks.

"I been wanting to tell you this I lo-"

Before he could finish his statement. Not even a second he flew across the room. As I glance to the person who did that. My eyes widen. But I ignored him and rapidly helped jungkook lying in the cold floor. As I touched his cheek he groan in pain and tried to stand up. But I didn't let him. Before something worst happen not worrying to jungkook but the man who decided to punched him. I know jungkook wouldn't let him getaway just like that But I decided to take care of it myself.

"What the fuck is wrong with you taehyung"

"He can't touched you like that that's why I punched him! No one can!" he shouted.

"I understand your just being protective but I know that's not the real reason why you suddenly punched him. You've been concealing this anger towards him.just tell me taehyung"

"Do you really wanna know" I nodded.

He walks towards me and when his close enough he gently lift my chin forcing me to look at him and he gave me a sweet peck on my lips making me close my eyes and be caught up in the moment. The kiss was short but I can still feel the passion and desire. As he pulled away but his lips still brushing against mine. And then I realize that we're not the only one in that place. I pushed him away from me and when i glance back to jungkook he wasn't there anymore.

"So yeon, I think I have have fallen for you"

"Jungkook" you breathily said his name.

"Don't worry about him just give him space and I'm sorry for not holding my self back. I shouldn't done that knowing that you already have feelings for someone and I know it's never gonna be me. But I didn't regret kissing you and telling you how I feel. I just want you too know that" he professed what's inside his heart but unfortunately you don't have the capacity to feel any sympathy for him after what he's done but you understand why he's feeling this type of way towards you. You played them not only them but their hearts for the special mission but theirs no regret not even one bit.

"Taehyung I'm sorry and if make you feel this way and please forget about me and tell that to jungkook. please don't ever try to find me. I have to go"

"So I'm never gonna see you ever again?"

I didn't even answer his question I just stormed off as fast as I can. Not caring where I'm going and bumping into. I just wanna be alone by myself right now. My mind is getting clouded so as my eyes. I need to get out of here.

□

Jungkook's POV

She dragged me outside and I just stared at her. She was telling me lies I know she felt the same way as I do for her. But doesn't wanna admit it. But I need to get my answers if she's not going tell me. I need to do something.

So I decided to kissed her. I felt it right then and there. By the way she kissed me it's full of love and passion. And the way she placed her hands at my chest. Feeling my heart beat. I already know what's her answer. But before I could actually tell her what I feel.

Taehyung decided to punch me I decided to punch him back but she stopped me. And then I saw them kissed right before my eyes. Which makes my heart tear into pieces. I thought she feel the same way. But I guess it was a lie again. I shouldn't trust her lying lips. That I have fallen over and over again. I can't bare see this. I decided to leave them alone.

□

Everyone gathered in the room. Namjoon's man finds and drag them back and tied them pointing a gun in right in their temples. excluding her. She can't be found. The tension in the atmosphere is getting thick again. Not until someone decided to speak.

"Drama aside. What's in your mind yoongi I can't seem to read it. Speak up or else you want your boys to get badly hurt"

"I don't want your help. I rather be broke and starve with them then rise up again without your help."

"You have no idea what I'm capable of don't test my patience suga, I've waited long enough for this day to finally happen and I'm not letting it go to waste"

"Not mentioning all of her efforts just to persuade you and your men who carelessly falls right into her beautiful traps, just using her pretty face isn't she the best"

"I don't give a shit of what you can do or what your capable of. Not even a beautiful spy can make me,I'm not involving me and my gang into your business again and your sickening obsession to take someone's lives. You killed them Just because they owe you something or their your rivals enemy."

I rather to be killed than to kill...

"You're no saint suga, your not different to us, we're all the same. You know I never take NO from anyone. I'm gonna let your boys live and give you time to think. I know this is a big decision to ponder about. But you already know I have my limits and you better say YES. And if you tried to runaway even if it's a foreign country. I'm gonna find a way to get you around my fingers again.

Consider yourselves lucky this time.

Chapter 17

"How did they found our new hideout there's no way in hell they could locate that so easily our IP address is impossible to find." Jimin let out his bottled frustration.

"That's not Important now, what matters is how the hell we didn't realize that's she's a freaking spy." Taehyung abruptly joining the conversation.

"Wait I think I know how they tracked us. Remember the day when she cooked dinner for us. While she's preparing the food I saw something shining behind her neck. But I didn't really mind it before but now I'm sure of it. It's a tracking device a small chip hidden underneath her hair." Jungkook started realising things he encountered before with her.

"You need to be so close to see that. does that mean your only centimeters away from her neck?" Jimin curiously asked with a tint of jealousy in his tone. "You could say that" jungkook said while gazing down from embarrassment.

"Because your too busy flirting with her and you jungkook what the hell was that about. Like what I said your too occupied with her. And because of that we have no where to go, we have no money and no food no nothing" yoongi complained at his younger members.

Yoongi leans his back at the rigid concrete wall and put his hands under his head he used this as a pillow. Even if it's really uncomfortable. He forced himself to sleep. He was tired and most of all stressed. He needs he's sleep and to rethink about namjoons persuasive offer. He already knows his answer but seeing the boys suffer like this a whole another story he really needs to make a decision before they end up dead either from starvation or wrong decisions.

□ □

Cmon suga you can do this. You just need to angle your gun to the side a little bit more and when you spot the target shoot him, Understand.

Gunshot sounds

Good your learning but it's gonna be difficult when you have to kill the real one, you need more practice but this will do at the close range.

What do you mean? I thought we're Learning this for self defense not to terminate a human being.

Oh I forgot to tell you that we also need this when we fight our opponent or people who doesn't learn their lessons.

This is morally wrong namjoon I don't wanna killInnocent people or any people unless is my last resort.

Their not that innocent their criminals and mafias that's the only way they will learn their lessons if they don't give us what we want. We take what's doesn't belong to them. Their lives...

Doesn't even fucking make sense we take their life for what? For drugs, money and privilege. We're not gods to take someone's life by placing a bullet through their heads.

We need to kill to survive this is not just for us it's for our gangs future and legacy, understood.

He just shook his head and put his focus on the shooting range. He decided to shrug off this thoughts and continue what's been done. Knowing that the youthful boys in his gang need to learn this type of torture at the very young age. All he knows is he doesn't wanna be doing this for all his life as job nor a sickening hobby.

□ □

You feel that your head is gonna explode with this tsunami of emotion running through you mind. It's filled with desire and temptation to leave namjoon's Gang and to be with the man you feel this strong waves of emotions for, The man who makes you realize that love does exists, The man who makes you feel like ecstasy every time his lips pressed against yours. The only man you felt interest for a very long time. Is the man in the white shirt. Even thought he hates you right now for kissing another man in front of him. But only him is all you can think about. The feelings that you never expose to him or revealed. You just wanna be with someone right now. You need to get this stress out of your tangled mind. Then your mind drifted you to someone, a friend of yours of a lifetime. Only Hoseok can make you feel better but he's with namjoon and you loathe him for his empty promises and he's stupid profound words when he's talking to you.

You opened your eyes slowly feeling your body heavy. The flight from Seoul to Jeju just started. As you stretch your self in this massive plane seat. It was first class and the food was really good the people were surprisingly nice and the service was great as well. But your doleful mood didn't change one bit because all you can think about is jungkook. And the brutality of your voice and the terrifying harsh truth you said to him. You're the one who pushed him away but your the one who also cannot stop thinking about him. You rested your head to the side as you tried to drift away from the this moment.

When the airplane landed while I was walking through the airport. I saw this man wearing all black. Black leather jacket, black pants, black beanie and a black bag. It reminds me of someone familiar but I couldn't really point out who it is. I decided to ignore it and continue on my way. When I reached the destined resort. I quickly go to my hotel room and dressed up. Suddenly I received a message on my mobile. I immediately take it out of my bag and answer the flooding messages.

[convo]

Hobi: Where the hell are you? So yeon I've been in your house and the cafe you always visited and your not there. You're making me really worried.

Sunny: I'm sorry hobi but I need a break but don't worry about me I'm still alive.

Hobi: Where are you I'm gonna get you there.

Sunny: No oppa please, I'm gonna be back soon, Don't you dare to follow me here.

Hobi: Arasso, just promise me you will come back.

Sunny: Yes I promise

He wouldn't mind if I enjoy my self first in this beautiful paradise before I came back to the stressful world I belong to. I really needed this. you opened the door and gracefully put a smile on your face.

When She walks outside, Suddenly she was the center of attention. All men and even woman are glancing at her direction. it seems like she makes everything stops and go in slow motion. As she slowly removes her sunglasses. Smiling at the people gazing at her. She glance up taking the warm sun rays as it hits her bare skin. While she take off her white lace cover up and gently strip it down to her body. Revealing the bright red two piece. That fits her body faultlessly.

She slowly get into the ocean feeling the slightly cold water touched her skin. Making her tensed body loosen in an instant. She swim under the blue water seeing all kinds of corals and fishes but she swam up because of the salty water and the deep waves crashing against her. She leisurely goes back to the shore. She puts both of her hands through her wet hair while getting out of water. Making all the men earlier gaze at her once again. She ignored the stares and go towards her chair and decided to sunbathe under the perfectly blazing sun and the tropical weather of the island that's she's been missing. She hears man and woman talking about her but none of the tried to approach her. So she stands up and glanced at them and gives them her fake smile leaving them speechless in their own tongues.

While walking back to your hotel room you harshly bump into someone. you apologize but the man just hurriedly run and left. You entered your room and change into your black lacy nightie. And gently rest your head to the soft pillow feeling the cloudy like material against your velvety skin. You close your eyes but you ended up opening it again. Your mind keep coming back to the man you bumped earlier. If he's a stalker he's really bad at stalking. Because you saw him three times first at the airport, second at the beach and lastly when you just bumped into him. but you decided to ignore the mysterious man instead. But it keeps bothering you. Nobody knows where you are not even your own best friend. Now your curious of who he could be. You thought it's gonna be fun to play with him for a little bit.

Does he have any idea who's the person he's stalking.

Chapter 18

She puts a silky robe on and head outside. She glanced around and see nobody. So she decided to get even further through the lighted pathway that goes to the shore. Suddenly She heard someone having a conversation on a phone and eavesdrop to the man talking behind the tall massive green bushes.

Hyung I can't see her getting stared by this disgusting man around her

Just get your ass back here

But I really wanna see her

You already did

Can't we just did what we did to her before

Stupid she's a fucking spy!

I heard it, you don't have to shout

Her eyes widen when she realize that the voice she's hearing is oddly familiar. For her to miss guess it. It was jungkook. Her thought got cut off by a strong grip with a cloth over her mouth. Before she pass out she kick his crouch area and then she falls in to the hard ground. The man just curse in his breath not wanting to make a loud noise and carried her somewhere.

I know it wouldn't be so easy to kidnapped you.

She felt really heavy like gravity is holding her down when she tried to lift her head upwards. She plop back down to the soft cushion and gave up. She decided to opened her eyes. Leaving her shock and confuse. She glance around the room and distinguish that she's never been here. But it seems familiar to her. She glance at the window and her eyes widen even more. She realize that she's not in jeju anymore. Perhaps she's was brought in by...

Before she could continue in her thoughts the door flew open revealing that man that kidnapped her.

"So yeon-ah you're awake, I'm sorry for doing this it's the order, but I have to-"

"Shut up Hoseok and don't talk to me"

"Forgive me, please don't do this to me. I kidnapped you because namjoon ordered me to I have no choice"

"No shit, argh my, my head is banging"

He immediately runs up to me and felt my forehead and he gently leave a soft peck. I was taken aback by what he did. But I remember that he always do this to me. When I'm frustrated or feeling down. I smiled to myself not realizing he's glancing at me with a big smile spread across his face. I couldn't fight the temptation now that's he's so close to me and my head is resting on his chest. I instantly gave him a hugged making him fall his back to the bed. And me hovering on top of him. We stayed there for a bit didn't realize were gazing at each other's orbs. I decided to sit back up and glance away. Sitting above his stomach. My knees position side to side. Not realizing someone is peering at us through the small gap. But the man suddenly opened the door fully and get inside the room.

"It's looks like you two are having a lot fun, but that's not what's suppose to happen"

"Seokjin it's not like that, you know I don't like him that way or this way and please stop staring at us it's embarrassing"

"No, I'm actually enjoying this, please don't go anywhere" Hoseok jokingly said.

"Shut your ass up Hoseok and lets get to work namjoons waiting in his office and don't forget to bring her with you" seokjin abruptly uttered.

He carried her by his shoulders and bring her to namjoons office. She has no energy so she just let Hoseok escort her to where there going. She still has no clue what's she doing here or why she's getting kidnapped by him and didn't just ask her like what normal people do. She doze of in his shoulder and her arms wraps around him.

While I was talking with yoongi on the phone. I heard someone gasped and muffled noises coming behind the bushes and when I follow the weird sounds. I didn't see anything. So I decided to go to her hotel room and when I sneak inside and opened her door. She was nowhere to be found. I hurriedly called yoongi and told him she's gone but all of her belongings are still there. He told me to get back home. When I get back to our temporary Place that we've been staying for the past few days. I go straight to Yoongi's room that we share and report to him what happens. But before I could opened the door it sounds like he's talking to someone by the phone. I figured because no ones answering back. But my eyes widen when I heard her name mention by Yoongi while talking to the other line furiously.

What am I so worried about her situation, I'm suppose to hate her from what she did to us.

Chapter 19

You felt your body gently being put an a rigid cushion. you suddenly woke up and realize that Hoseok suppose to bring you in Namjoons office. As you heard someone cleared there throat beside your ears. Making you fully awake and peered at the person in front of you. He's eyes are quite terrifying like he's trying to threaten you or something but you lean your face even closer to his. displaying the same intense glare at him.

"I'm not scared of you namjoon, I'm sorry if that's what your thinking" I whispered.

"I know that very well. That's why I ordered to kidnapped you because if I threaten to kill one of the boy you love. You wouldn't believe me unless I show it to you"

"You don't have to and I'm here already. So why in hell did you kidnapped me for?"

"Well your mission is not done yet So yeon this is just the beginning. Plus you didn't do a good job by having an affair with one of our hostile and you broke the rules missy. You know your gonna get consequences for that. But I'm a fairly nice guy. I'm not giving you your punishment but instead you have to do this final assignment. you wanna see your brother right? This is your last chance"

He handed me a black folder. I hesitate before grabbing it. I stared at it for a bit and gathered myself together for what I'm about to see. when I finally opened it my eyes grew in shock. Seeing the names of the people listed in the paper he obligated me in the rearmost duty. All of a sudden it brings back all the memories that I hardly erased in my mind. But it keep coming back trying to destroy me once again. I was pulled back to earth when someone tapped my shoulder. I peer at him and then back at namjoon.

"But my job it's done. you already get all their money and destroy their home including their life. What else do you want from them?"

"I want them back as our alliance and only you can do that. Not only for our gangs future but to continue its legacy. Don't take chances So yeon this is your only way to prove me why I choose you specifically to do this complex mission. Rather than our best spies in this company. Choose wisely"

"I accept it"

Wait did I really accept his offer. Just do this for your brother and noting else. I can do this.

Good girl...

"Just so you know I'm not doing this for you nor for your gang, I'm doing this for myself don't get that wrong"

He chuckled. "don't worry I'm aware"

"What should I do for them to believe me continually?"

"In fact, You don't need to do anything just be you that's all they want. They want you..."

"They want what!? Are you selling me now namjoon is this what this is, what if I don't get out there alive!" I shouted at his face with my large eye glaring at him scarily.

"Not exactly but some sources told me that two of them is madly in love also with one of my strikingly gorgeous spy. Instead of getting furious. Why not use this as our advantage, right hoseok?" He nodded as he agreed to disagree at his boss.

"What exactly do you want me to do?"

"This is the important part that you missed. While you were minding your own world and no where to be found. Listen carefully I don't like repeating myself. The Bangs and The Tans are once together, but this bastards decided to betray us and create their own gang. Not that there heavily needed to ours. But why not Pursue them and bring back Bangtan the former most feared and powerful gang in the modern Korea. The chore that I particularly assigned you. Is to pretend that we kidnapped you and used you for ransom. We don't their need money, We need them. Your job is to convince them to recede back to us. Be as petty as you can. I don't care I want them as quick as a lightning. I'll give you one day to finish this work and then we can talk about what you want as a prize"

"Are you kidding you want me to finish this mission in just 24 hours that's impossible"

"Not with you missy that's why I entrust you to do this business, Because I believe in you" he gaze at me like he's challenging me with a proud expression he has. I took a deep breath and pressed my back at the firm couch as I closed my eyes and think deeply. If I made the right decisions. There's no turning back. I'm gonna be surprise if they still believe my dexterity acting despite of betraying them before.

"Are you done over there!" Hoseok shouted outside the bathroom while handling the rope and the black fabric bag in his hands.

"I just need to fix my fake bruises I'll be out in a minute" she shouted back at the man that sounded like a muffled noise because she inside the four walled space. She got out of the bathroom and i stared at her and then mess her hair even more. She turn around for him to tied her hands back with a rope and before he put a burlap sack over her head. she turn back facing him. He unintentionally wraps his arms to her waist and embrace her backwards.

"Hoseok what are you trying to do. stop this before I change my mind" I plead at him with a maddening tone in my voice.

"I'm sorry So yeon, You don't have to do this just tell me and I'll talk to namjoon. I'll try to convince him somehow. I just don't want you to get hurt again"

"Hobi don't worry about me. I can take care of myself okay. You know what, Just give me a peck on my forehead as a good luck charm like you always do"

He flashes me one of his angelic smiles and kissed my forehead tenderly with his soft lips. I closed your eyes tendering the last moment with him. After that I suddenly felt a soft thing landed on my lips as well. He planted a small but sweet peck on my lips. Making my eyes widen and glare at him with an seriously expression plastered on my face.

"Yah! Jung Hoseok I'm punishing you after I get out of this, I'm going to beat you to pulp after stealing a kiss from me!"

She see nothing just darkness surrounding her and only white noise can be heard. She's been sitting in this broken chair for half an hour now just waiting for something to occur. Not until she heard the door creaked open and a person gasped deeply. Not a second passed she was being embraced tightly by this unknown man. She felt the Black bag being taken off her head as the lights slightly blind her. She instantly lift her hands to cover her eyes but then she remembers it was still tied up behind her back. As she felt the man cut the rope in her wrist finally making her hands breathe from the tight grip around it. Before she could feel her hands he already grasp it and rub in gently. Making her glance at him and then back at her slightly bruised hands.

"Does it still hurt, I'm sorry if I take too long to come. I thought I would never see you ever again. now that your here I will never let you go, Even if namjoon get furious, I wouldn't care, You will be with us forever"

What the hell is he talking about?

"I appreciate you coming back yoongi just to save me and I apologize for what happened the last time. I was threaten to do that mission. They said that they will kill my br-"

"Don't worry your safe now So yeon, we're finally gonna be together. you have us and only you can trust is us do you understand." You faked your smile as you looked at him in a comfortable warmth with your eyes. He glanced back at you with his most genuine gaze that you don't feel anything for. Your numb and no can make you trust them even if they begged you.

I don't trust anyone and no one trust me.

Chapter 20

I already gave you the time that you deserve and where's my answer yoongi?

Like I already said I want her back with us I don't give a shit if she's a spy. I want her away from you. You evil creature. She's going with me and after that you can get what you want from us.

She's not that innocent as you think she is Because that's all she showed, her being such a valiant girl is for me and for my gang only. I'm not giving her up for you to play her as a toy.

Namjoon did you forgot your the bad guy here not me. So don't flip the script.

Well to be honest she's not working for me anymore she just left us including this town But I can grasp her if i want to. Let's make a deal. Sign this contract and both of us get what we want.

He sighed deeply. Hand me the contract?

Don't fear I'm gonna find your most prize possession and bring her back well and alive.

What a bastard. He curse in his breath

He lost in his train of thoughts when he heard her mention his name. He glimpse at her and then dart his eyes back at the null road.

"Yoongi are you alright, you seem so quiet it's scaring me. Are we near to our destination it's looks droughty like a desert out here"

"Pardon me I was just lost in my own thoughts, don't sweat were not that far"

"Can I ask you a question?"

"You can ask anything you want princess"

"Can I ask you a favor? Can you stop calling me that, but I'm not your princess anymore"

"What makes you say so? I adore calling you that. I don't really like calling people their real name, plus it suits you, dainty but fragile and also can be a badass if she wanted too"

"Stop stealing Jimin's lines. it's weird if it's coming from you. I'm not used to it"

"What's your question then, Ask away" still focus on the rough route.

"It's very simple why did you trust me again"

He heed at me once again the sincerity of his eyes. He's vast stares is slowly distracting me from my plans. I don't know if I'm ready to hear what he's about to say. His gaze is back at the turnpike as he speaks.

I was abandoned by my mother at a very young age. My father is the only one that supports me. But he can't be with me because my mom is just a used woman and gave birth to me as a mistake. He has his own happy family. I remember he has a daughter a little younger than my age. I met her once before she was so adorable. But she always have nightmares just like you. I was so happy that I have a sister but not until father stop visiting, I didn't see him for a month whilst he never forgets to come by and see me every week sometimes with my step sister. But this one day my mother sadly break the devastating news that he was brutally murdered with his wife and fortunately the kid was safe and wasn't harmed. But after that I've never heard of her, Of my mother she left me alone and afraid. Including her my little sister I never saw her again since that tragic incident. A teenage boy lonesome on his own without anyone to take care and support him emotionally and mentally. I became doleful and lonely not even because of my own parents leaving me but I became like this because of her. Ive known this girl very well despite of meeting her a few times. It felt like the half of me is gone. Along with my light and happiness.

Not longer when I met namjoon and his gang they brought light into my life but it didn't last. I'm not born to destroy and most of all to croak people. But I have no choice at the time. he brought me here in this position without any doubt in my ability to he his second hand. I don't want you to be tormented at the end. Things will come back to you like a tornado and there's no way you can obstruct it. You will become miserable. I'm gratified for having the maknaes they always find a way to brighten my darkest days. You know you've been affected too by their merriness and humorous antics that's actually makes them stand out from the rest. but I'm warning you things can get rough and addictive in his gang. Of I were you I wanna stop myself before it's too late.

You are speechless after his long admiring speech about his past life and his boys that stick with him even when the worst days of his life occurred. Your still star stuck at him. You're in awe, not knowing what to say or do. He chuckled and leans closer to your face getting your attention on him.

"I know thats a lot to absorb in one day. But you don't have to stare at me like that"

"W-What are you doing yoongi" Wait why am I stuttering. He leaned even nigher towards your face as you looked away avoiding his strong gaze not helping his face are also merely inches away from yours.

He just chuckled and unclasp the seatbelt at the side of your waist and lean back up to his seat. He turns off the engine and get out of the car. Not even a second you heard a knock on you window. Making you flinched. As he opened the car door and offering you his milky soft hands. You gladly accept it without realizing. He gently pulled you out of the vehicle. You quietly trails behind him peering downwards. He suddenly speaks, lending your undivided attention to him. As you met his gaze.

You saw a small old cabin in the middle of the woods. You glimpse a the person waving his tiny hands inside the lodge. As you walked your way their, the door slams open. And the person suddenly hugs you. Making you instantly melt from his touch. You slowly return the hug. As you felt him smile at the crook of your neck. The man hugged you for awhile earning looks from the boys across the room. You broke the hug and cupped his cheeks giving him your genuine smile. You saw his face get red in an instant. Leaving him in utter shock.

"Jiminie your hands are still in my waist pabo"

"I'm sorry, I just missed you, I mean we missed you. What happen to you, let's get you dressed up and then supper after you freshen up"

Before I could shift, another pair of arms wrapped around mine. As I did the same to him and patted his back softly. He glance at me with his hazelnut hue orbs telling me how cared and longed for me and my touch.

"Taehyung stop looking at me like that your making my face red" Making him blush even more. Showing me his endearing box smile.

"Don't you ever leave us again, I really thought I would never see you again, but you're here. Ive never been be happier"

You leered up and you saw him. You made eye contact for split seconds. But you avert your gaze somewhere else. The man you wanna see the least, The man you've been longing for, The man you've been seeing even in your dreams, The man who suppose to fall into your pitfall but instead you fall into his. And the man you can't even looked to his alluring dark orbs. That you've been craving to gaze forevermore. Since your eyes landed on him. You can't seem to see anyone else. You been entrapped into his spell. That you never wanna get release from. It's too beautiful to farewell. But what your feeling is not ideal to the world you choose to be a part of. At the end of the day that man is still jungkook one of your gangs nemesis.

"Where can I see the bathroom?" You query trying to avoid him and to escape his strong gaze upon your direction.

"It's in the left corner next to your room, We already prepare what your gonna wear it's all in your room" yoongi spoke with a slightly smile on his face.

You seat in between yoongi and taehyung.Because you wanna be as far as you can from jungkook. You don't wanna make the great atmosphere died down and destroy your last moment with the boys. Before bewitching them again with your plans, That you were force to.

"Lets cheers now that she's back with us" jungkook said while his eyes still peering at you rigorously with a sly smirk on his face. Loving your uncomfortable figure under his gaze.

You heard the wine glass clanks together as they said their cheers and glance at your direction. You gave them your fake smile that they seem to believe it was genuine. They continue to toast but this time your joined them in their facade. You sip into your glass contains of red colored liquid, hiding the smirk plastered across the pretty face of yours.

Why don't I feel bad for deceiving them once again...Call me the bad guy...But instead it excites me even more...

Chapter 21

You walked out of the bathroom while tying up your brown locks into a messy bun and stand there leaning your body at the door frame wearing a oversized white shirt. You crossed your arms as you step forward one of your long slightly tanned legs making it shines under the moonlight. As you peek at the four man still focusing at the small bright screen of the old television. You cleared your throat gaining all their attention into you. You saw their eyes widen by the stunning view of yours. You chucked at their reaction and walked inside the room. You feel their eyes following every movement you do. Until you sit next to yoongi and lightly tap his thigh. You saw disappointment hidden behind their straight face.

"Yoongi can I talk to you in private if that's alright with you?" I glance at him with my dewy eyes. "Why not talk here we wanna know what your gonna say" jungkook spat. "He's right, plus this is a small house you can hear everything. theirs no such thing as private" yoongi uttered and gaze back at me. "I just feel uncomfortable knowing one of your members doesn't want me here" you said heeding back at yoongi. But then you heard a low chuckled coming from the arrogant man that's been ignoring you since you came. "Who? Jungkook, don't mind him he's just like that, Everyone loves I mean like you here. I apologize on my behalf if he makes you feel some type of way" yoongi reassured you. you gave him a faint smile in return.

"What do you wanna talk about, do you mind telling us too" taehyung said earning a slap at his shoulders by one his Hyungs. "Didn't she said it was private, but why does it need to be yoongi you can share me your thoughts if want too" jimin asked. "You're the same as me" Taehyung uttered "I choose yoongi to talk to because he would give me a biased opinion and give me a real answer. Rather than talking to both you" They both said in unison "we can be smart like Hyung too" you chucked. "I don't know what to do without you two" Making their pouty faces lit up instantly. "Now listen to me, I don't know what exactly namjoon and his gang did to yours but all I want is peace and I don't wanna get involved and fight anymore it's so tiring. But now that I'm in this position that my own people flipped on me and captured me as a bait. My only wish is too fix the mess they started. Not by them but by your people" I said slowly convincing them to side on me.

"But how do we know your not lying again. We know you're the best actress out here" jungkook sternly said. "If I need to get undress and naked for you to see that I don't have anything attached on me. I will, just for you to believe me. I know it's a slow process to gain someone's trust but where am I right now. I'm here aren't I, Give me another chance" You said with pleading eyes, you hold Yoongi's hand tightly. Because you know his toughest one to believe you beside jungkook. The other two is can be easily persuade.

Yoongi nodded as a agreement at your compelling plead. You turn around at the two man behind you. You casually rest your hands on top Jimin's thigh and looked straight into his glistening orbs. Trying to manifest him to believe in you. He hesitated at first but he smiled back assuring you. You sat beside taehyung and held His face cupping his gently cheeks. You gaze at him depthless. You used your eyes as a sign that you're telling the facticity and make all of them fall in your ploy once again. "So yeon is your shooting for a movie done already, you're taking so much of my time if you mind I will to get out here" jungkook sarcastically said.

"I know I can't please everyone, even if I try my best. Don't fear I will not be bothered by it" You sadly said. "What did I say earlier don't mind him, his not the one who control us. I'm the leader here so do as I say and you Jungkook you're not going anywhere" you suddenly wraps your arms around him hugging him he instantly return it back. You felt a sly smirk crept up to your lips as you felt the nigh victory. Even though one of them doesn't buy your dexterous acting skills. You didn't seem to be bothered about him. Three is enough to get this mission into a success.

You heard him leave as the wooden door swing closed with a loud bang. You remove yourself from yoongi as you eyes was stuck at the door. "I need to follow and talk to him" you said while you get up from the couch and run towards where jungkook headed earlier. Not giving them a chance to protest. You rapidly trail behind him despite of just wearing an oversized shirt in a cold night. You couldn't catch up to him he was to fast for your sprinting abilities like he's a professional runner. You stoped your tracks panting softly trying to catch your breath. As you felt your hands gets dragged Pulling you inside the dark eerie woods. You easily get out of the grip because it was too loose. You held his wrist tightly with force and roughly turn it around over his head. As your knees get contact with his stomach. He groans in pain as he surrender. you waited a few seconds before loosening your grip to sense that he really gave up and then finally letting the man go. You saw the light coming from the moon shines brightly upon his facial features. Your eyes grew in shock as you rethink your actions a second ago. you realise the man you attack is noting like a foe.

"I surrender, I shouldn't done that. I must forgotten how fatal you can be, I've been warned but still didn't listen to hoseok"

"Forgive me namjoon, I mean boss it's just my instinct to defense myself when I feel like I'm in danger. I'll be careful next time"

"I understand, but can you help stand upYou did quite a damage but I'm still intactThank godness you didn't put your full force to me or else it's gonna be worst than this"

"My apologies"

"Now, why I'm here is about the mission. is it going well as I wanted it to be. You only got few more hours to convince them and to make their final decision"

"Yes I'm done with the three. One more to go. I swear his a freaking rock he's emotionless I couldn't manipulate him believe in me but I'm doing my best that I can at the current situation"

"That's what I like, you never give up and always find your ways even if your risking that precious pride you have"

"I need to head back before they notice I've been gone for too long, I'll report to you when the morning comes and please don't come up to me like that again"

"Understood, you may take your leave"

You rapidly head back smoothy inside the house without making any noise. You opened the door to your settled room and enclosed it lightly. When you turned around you were faced with the man you least expected. Your only inches away from each other's features. You can hear the loud beating of his heart. Entailed with yours too beating in sync.

"Jungkook How did you get here, I was about to follow you but yo-" he coldly cut your words.

"I don't wanna hear anything that comes out of your mouth, that lying...lips of yours"

I might have to do something you can't resist

You leaned you face closer to his leaving invisible gap between you two. You softly brush yours against his luscious lips. You felt his breath hitch from the sudden closeness.

"Why are you stoping yourself go and kiss me right now" you whispered in his lips tempting him to make the bold move.

He leans even closer as your lips touched but he suddenly pulled away from yours. Then He groan in annoyance. He looked away and out of no where punched the old fragile door beside you making you flinch. As you heard the boys wake up and runs towards the loud sound he created. "What's happening behind there So yeon, opened the door. How did you even came back without us noticing" you broke your intense stare off and slowly open the door revealing you and jungkook.

"Is everything okay?" They all said in unison

"Yes everything's is perfectly fine" you replied

"Have both of you already discused about it, because when the morning comes we're leaving this old cabin and we're gonna live with namjoon, I made up my mind she's right and the two of them agreed already" you felt a tiny smirk slowly crept to your lips.

"Are you really believing what this woman said I'm not leaving this place and most of all not with that bastard, I'm not going, I'm staying"

"Were left with no choice, he's cutting our resources, A day or two and we're left with nothing again. I'm not doing this for her nor for him but for us. Can't you sense that?" yoongi said with anger towards the young lad.

"Are you already giving up Hyung, what's for? all our sacrifices and hard work we've done in the past year. Your just gonna throw that away Including your little pride"

"This is just temporary, I don't see us get along with each other either but what important is now, we need to eat and a place to stay and we're also bringing her to live with us"

"Let's not fight and deal with current situation which is tomorrow it's gonna be a big day, our lives might change forever for the good" jimin replied.

"I'm finally gonna taste seokjin's food, I've been waiting for a whole year" Taehyung said changing the atmosphere into a light one.

You chuckled softly but hid it vaguely. Jimin hit taehyung at the back of his head earning a grunt from him. You saw yoongi slightly smile as his reaction to the two children's bickering. You glance at jungkook he just shook his head disagreeing with the decision their leader has finally made. But he has no choice but to accept it wholeheartedly even if it's opposite to what he intended to do.

Chapter 22

You opened the minivan's doorway while jimin offers his adorable hands gesturing for you to hold it. As you grabbed his hands you glanced at the luxurious mansion where you and namjoon's gang lives. You were welcomed by the luscious green bushes perfectly alined all over the extravagant house. You looked around as you felt yourself smile seeing the boys jaw dropped as a reaction gazing at the new place there gonna be living in henceforth. You turn to your left and see your boss namjoon standing tall towering you giving you a ecstatic gaze that couldn't be hidden across his face. You smiled back at him and back to your poker face as fast as it occurred.

He gestured all of you too head inside his mansion. When you entered inwards. You saw him suddenly runs up to you and gives you the tightest embrace that he could produce. Showing that he really did missed you to that extent. But you decided not to return the warm hug he lended to you. Whereas you don't want the boys behind you too get suspicious than they already is. Instead you slowly withdraw from his arms and go towards the boys and hid yourself behind them not realizing it's was Jungkook not that you have a choice but because he's the nearest to you.

"Hey So yeon it's okay, there not gonna hurt you were here to protect you" he hid me even more at his back. You were taken aback by his sudden kindness towards you. It makes your heart jumps from his simple touch.

"I'm sorry if you still feel uncomfortable around me. I will make my self up next time" Hoseok said with his caring tone feeling guilt of what he cause you to pulled away from his hugs that he knows well you always craved from him after a long day. When you rejected him it makes him genuinely gloomy inside.

"It's fine I just get startled when you suddenly hugged me, aside from that I'm fine now"

"Well let me show you where your designated room is. We better start now this is a huge house to start with" seokjin said to break the building tension.

When you reached your room after jin showing the boys there room. before you can turn the knob if the door. Out of no where someone wraps their arms around your petite body back hugging you. You purses your lips together knowing the person who's behind you is Hoseok. He must felt terrible earlier by the way you acted towards him. You turn yourself to face him and glance around if there's anyone. Nothing. You unexpectedly enfold your arms around him. Nuzzling your head to his soft chest. You felt a smile being created in his charming face.

"I knew it, you will never get mad from me without a valid reason" he withdraw from the hug and kissed your forehead gently. You Softly smiled at him gazing at each other. Only you got distracted from your mutual bonding with your long lost friend when someone vociferate your whole name from a distant. "Park so yeon!" You're instinct turned your body to that direction and sight taehyung standing next to your room. His gaze is full of rage and jealousy towards the both of you. You glides over taehyung. You left him knowing he understand your sudden change of personality. You bring him inside his massive dark painted room. You hushed him by gazing mildly through his brown glistening orbs. You know he can't resist your pleasing eyes that's makes him softened promptly. Just by giving your undivided attention to him. You decided to speak when he finally calmed down.

"Taehyung why did you called me for"

"Who does he think he is, and why are you looking at him like you didn't seen him in forever, You even hugged him. So yeon, I don't know who to believe anymore"

"It's all misunderstanding taehyung, Listen the person who you need to believe is me"

"I don't know there's too much in my mind right now" he gaze away from your alluring eyes that he always get lost to. Before you can protest someone speaks through the speaker connected to all rooms in the whole house. We heard Jin's voice rang to our ears. Calling us to go down for supper.

"It's a early dinner, I wonder why maybe namjoon need to announce something"

You dart at taehyung still stuck inside his thoughts. You slowly intertwined you hands to his. Establishing his doubts towards you. He held your hands tightly and gander at you certitude about your statement early on. You both head to the dining hall and go find yourselves a seat. Taehyung signaling you to seat in between him and jungkook. You gladly followed him.

First move to gain someone's trust is by giving them your earnest loyalty

"There you are, what are you waiting for eat up before the food that I specially cooked gets cold" seokjin said breaking the thick atmosphere.

They glance at each other and nods before indulging in the delicious supper seokjin specifically prepared for their anticipated reunion. They haven't share a meal before since a year ago before their relationship went on a rough path. That cause them to break the gang apart. Feasting in this table will be dissimilar from now on. But they have to discard all their loathness to one another. To accomplished what both sides wanted.Which happens to be tranquility once and for all.

"Hyung thank you for the delicious dinner I've been craving your cooking for so long and now it finally happened" he uttered

"Taehyung-ssi I missed your compliment towards the food I created my masterpiece, namjoon and Hoseok don't really appreciate it that much only the maknaes always praise my excellent cooking skills" he laugh after he finished the sentence. Instantly affecting the whole area making the boys chucked in unison. Not because it's hilarious but it's new to see them all giddy and laughing with each other.

After the splendid time you shared with them. You disappear from their sight and sneak into namjoon's office. When you got there you were surprised by seokjin laying comfortably at the massive Maxwell couch while his feet dangling from the other side. Whereas the long legged man with a slender body and a broad shoulders. He noticed your existence and gesture you to sit beside him.

"I need to have a talk with namjoon but I can't seem to find him anywhere, do you perhaps know were he is"

"He left not too long ago, you know he's always busy working, I'm sure he's going back some time soon, you can tell me instead"

"If you insist, well I have two questions and the first one only namjoon can answer. So I guess I'm left with the second one" I sighed before continuing. "umm it's about the boys, I know you have heard of this but they like me no they love me"

"I'm aware namjoon told me about this, I think it's infatuation, you share the same age with some of them. There's just curious about you, Answer me honestly, do you fancy one of them"

"Seokjin-ssi, I'm not sure of what I feel, don't worry I can still reach the surface, I'm not deeply immerse with any of them yet... And don't tell this to anyone please not even namjoon or I'll be in dead meat"

"I understand, this is personal matter after all, he will not know a thing aside from that we need to stop them and most of all you missy or else we're gonna get in such trouble"

"I know and I'm apologize for my act lately"

"I got an brilliant idea, earlier I saw how they got so defensive or should I say Jealous when Hoseok is near you"

"What exactly are you planning?"

"Why not use him as your pretend lover. It's gonna be interesting to watch all of them get overprotective over you. Don't worry it's gonna be fun plus it's a little boring here a simple experiment won't hurt"

I'm not entirely sure about that brilliant idea your implying.

Chapter 23

The morning fell abruptly. The rush of memories from last night keep bugging in your head. You grasp back the eventful happenings. You have to pretend to be lovers with your pal for them to layover their devotion towards you. You broke your thoughts when you heard a loud knock on your door. You get up and opened it with a slow pace. You peek your head to the slight gap. You were befuddle by Hoseok standing inches away from your face. You stumbled back. Making the door fully opened. He closed the passage behind him and leer at you.

"Are you sure about this, Seokjin Hyung told me about the situation you have and I agreed to it, but if you don't want it's totally fine."

"I've made up my mind, this is the only way they will stop bothering me" You paused before continuing. "I never thought I will ever do this to my best friend. Hobi will you be my boyfriend?"

He stared at me for awhile and he bursted out from laughing at my unreal confession. You joined him after. He suddenly cough from cackling so hard.

"I should be the one who's asking you that, but that was adorable coming from your mouth. I'm just not used to it I guess."

"Never mind, where's namjoon I have to talk to him about some stuff" I asked.

"You already know where he is" he said.

You entered his office and closed the door behind you. You sat across him as he placed a new black folder in front of you. You glared at him and back to the confidential files. You sighed as you scan the context printed in the white bond paper.

"Before we start I congratulate you for putting the mission into a triumph. The second part of it starts the day after this. your gonna be paired with jimin AKA your husband and Hoseok will be the one to monitor the target and the rest is in the concluded in the black folder."

"May I interfere with the plan, is it possible to switch Hoseok to be my beloved husband perhaps. I'm more comfortable around him."

"You know Jimin is the charmer in this group and Hoseok isn't really a flirty kinda guy" I looked at him with pleading orbs.

"I'll give you a pass since the last job I gave to you is a success and don't disappoint me" he uttered "I promise."

When you get out of the office you saw Hoseok patiently waiting for you outside. Like a actual gentleman would. You grab a hold of his hands startling him quite a bit. You dragged him to the dining hall where all of us gathered to eat. When the both of you stepped inside the loud atmosphere of them earlier cackling and chatting with each other died down. And all of the sudden their eyes are on you. You remove your grasp to Hoseok and find yourself a seat. Of course you sat beside your fake admirer. You ignore their sharp stares and proceed to want your intended to do at the first place. Making them envious about your inevitable relationship scene with Hoseok.

"Let's start eating, shall we" seokjin breaks the ice.

"Woah, the food looks amazing I bet taste as it looks" taehyung said in amusement.

"I'm starving already let's dig in" he said.

You saw Hoseok picking up the smoking grilled meat by chopsticks and started feeding you. You hesitate at first but eventually gave in to his romantic gesture and eventually joined his playacting. You gladly ate the flavorsome spoonful he offered. Earning looks from the boys around the massive table. The show carry through not until someone decided to speak up. Both of You sighted the person and then look back at each other sharing a tiny smirk plastered across your faces.

"Would you mind explaining what we're witnessing in front of us this weird tension is slowly killing me" yoongi asked.

"Yesterday you couldn't even look at him in the eyes but now your being lovey dovey around him?" Jimin uttered with pint of jealousy in his tone.

"What's really between you two?" Taehyung added to the thickening conversation earning nods to the people across the table.

"We have a past... relationship, that's why I feel uneasy near him but earlier we manage to talked it out" your quickly to respond to their questions.

"Are you implying that you fixed the things that's been going on with you two in the pass" seokjin replied making it believable.

"Are you back together now?" Yoongi said still shocked at the current situation. The both of you nodded at his statement while gazing down hiding the grin in your faces.

"Unbelievable, What is this shtick your playing so yeon" jungkook interrupts the moment as his mellow eyes started to change.

"Why do you always talk to her with such high tone in your voice, you jealous?" Hoseok added to change the topic.

"I have no time for this nonsense, I'm done eating, I lost my appetite" he bows to the eldest members and left the table. Jimin stood up to follow him but you blocked him.

"It's my cause and I'm fixing it" you trailed where jungkook disappeared.

You gently closed the double door behind. You sighted jungkook laying his back in his canny bed looking undisturbed his eyes is stuck in the ceiling. Before you can speak he stood up and sauntered upon you. You stepped back by the sudden closeness. He has this maddening smirk plastered across his refined face. He chucked in vanquish for Intimidating you. Not until he break the tension and speak.

"What do you want, why don't you go back there to your man Hoseok but instead you're here, now you want to play me" he leans his face nigh to yours staring at your features. You can feel his eyes tracing your pinkish lips before he gazing back at your eyes.

"Jungkook can't you talk a little further away your uncomfortably close" you ended saying in a whisper.

"Put my name in your mouth again and I will crashed my lips into that cherry lips of yours."

There's a stray lines of protest that wanna come out of my mouth but something stopping you but you need to preach him.

"Jungkook" he stared at me with such domineering yet adoring filled eyes. After that he gently placed his hands at the side of my head and then down on my chin faintly lifting it up until our gaze met. But you didn't let him. Which makes him use a bit of force to make you look at him. Then both of our lips crashed together. He kissed me delicately at first then it becomes rough when started biting my lips. As he moves down on to my jawline and my collarbone leaving wet kisses all over it. Likes he's a famished tiger that haven't eaten in eternity. Your hands suddenly got contact at his face. Slapping him. He stoped touching the

Reddening area. He chuckled low and poke his tongue at the side of his cheeks.

"Jungkook that was not love that was vengeance"

"You knew but still you always tried to provoke me, look what your doing to me So yeon you're making me crazy."

"Stop that... stop your heart please nothing good is gonna come out of this conversation I need to go" I said trying to avoid him this discussion. he holds my wrist but before he could do much further somebody grabbed my other hand and pulled it hiding me behind his broad body. I felt relieved even though I don't know who just saved me.

"Taehyung, Why are you here? Stop interfering can you" jungkook said while walking over to us.

"Didn't we talked about this that you can't have her the way you wanted unless she felt the same way."

"She does though" he replied with a cocky tone in his voice "but that's not what it looks like. Can't you see she shaking she's fearful by you. Don't come near her again or else Hyungs will know"

He nods contradicting to whats in his mind. "Get lost before I change my mind."

Not even split seconds taehyung manage to bring you in his room. Prior to you turning you body to his direction. He unlikely enfold you around his broad arms. Feeling warmth and security through his embrace. You rested your head on his firm shoulders. You heard a light chuckle escaped his lips.

"Taehyung...I just wanna say...Thank you"

"I'll escort you to your bedroom, you seem tired, we'll talk some other time, I'll pay a visit in your room by dinner if you allow me too. But for now take a rest" you nodded as you both walked in front of your room.

"I'm lucky to have someone like you, tae" You felt him grinned behind you. As he broke the hug and walked his way towards the exit.

"By the way namjoon left something for you I've placed it in your nightstand."

Your hand ghosted at the silver knob and faintly opened the cabinetry making a small creaking sound. You begin looking for what's namjoon's have in the store for you. You picked up the black folder and rested it on top of your lap. But something caught your eyes. A long shaped metal shining brightly inside the dark filled hutch neatly placed underneath the grey clothing above it. You reached for the glistening object. You held it firmly in your hands as you turn it upside down. You saw a initial engraved beautifully into it.

J.JK

As you recurred the memories back then when you trespassed their hidden chamber and stole a gun not included in your mission but you need it protect your self and well being. From their non evil selves. You lightly remove the collected dust with your fingers aloft it. A small smile rested on your face knowing that he withhold this exquisite pistol and this is his prized possession. You position it back to the grey colored fabric and enclosed the cupboard. The lamp lit up by your command as you slid back to your bed and hold the paper firmly in your fingers. But you got jumbled in your thoughts.

As your fingers reached for your lips, all you can think about is him.

Chapter 24

You glance at your reflection in the largish mirror. You move the dress slightly to the side revealing your stunning long legs one of your best features. You turn around to sight your whole look. The long magenta gown made of expensive silky material encrusted with Swarovski placed nicely at the neck line. Displaying your alluring back and your slender arms. Showing off a lot of your flawless skin but enough to shield your chest and exceptional areas. The dress is elegant yet sultry. The detailed fabric that hugs your tiny waist tightly giving you gorgeous curves you didn't know existed. You got distracted from your thoughts when someone knocks at the woodwork. Then it opens exposing Hoseok in his fancy tuxedo that fit his body looking ravishing as well.

"Do I look good? it's quite seductive isn't it"

You did a little spin for him showing all of the lavishness of the thin fabric. That they called attire that you wear when your invited in a prestige event like we're attending in a few moments.

"You look really beautiful So yeon" he replied in amusement. "Let's head down stairs shall we" he nods and you trailed behind him. When you reach the bottom staircase you glanced up meeting his gaze. He looks drop dead in all black suit with his newly black hair slicked back. He waved his hands in front of your face. You snap at your daze. And dart your eyes avoiding his gaze.

"Do I look that good looking that you couldn't take your eyes away from me" you looked back.

"Of course not, your tie is unassembledLet me fix it quickly. You don't wanna look unpresentable to the place were going"

Jimin nods gesturing you to fix the flaws he didn't even noticed. You leans closer to him. you move near to the crook of his neck enable to straighten the tangled fabric. You engulf his strong intoxicating perfume. That he probably used to lure the prey. You knowing that it doesn't affect you. You shift nearer as you felt him gulped thickly. You pulled away and lastly touched the tie from his neck to his hard chest making his body tensed up. "Done you looked even better with my signature touch to it" you wink at him leaving him stunned. You held your sumptuous dress up and go on your way to find Hoseok.

"Are you prepared your gonna witness her magic when it comes to this type of stuff"

"Braced yourself and watch both of us blow your mind"

The limousines door opens, Hoseok offered his hands and you gladly accept it. as you walked in the blue carpet. ocean of paparazzi overflowing the entire venue. The man in a suit asked for an invitation. He smiled at them as he handed them the golden envelope. He check if it's authentic. Then He let us inside the blue house. It's like the White House but in the country of Korea. The mansion almost looked like a castle from its luxurious interior and extravagant furniture pieces that believed to come from the past dynasty that been kept and preserved well through out the century. It has this classic Korean design yet modern American fusion to it. You gaze at Hoseok gesturing him that someone is approaching us.

"Good evening, are you enjoying yourselves so far?" A Middle aged man greeted us with a lavish smile.

"We love the atmosphere and the luxuriant feel of the masnion" you answered confidently mirroring the smile on his face.

"By the way I'm Han ju seok and she's Han min na my stunning fiancé, isn't she looks gorgeous tonight with this red dress she's wearing"

"Indeed, you are very lucky, it's my pleasure to meet you two, looks like the young couple of a prestige Han family has arrived, well please suit your selves"

"Will do, it's a pleasure to meet you too"

The man left the both of you in tranquil. "Did he said suit our selves, gladly mister" you sternly said earning a side glance from Hoseok. As you heard jimin speaking in the earpiece you hid vaguely beneath your hair.

"I've located the target he's right there the old man in the corner of the room. Seated in the red velvety couch, wearing a full white tux, kinda balding" You chucked at his last statement. But you hid it briskly. As you gathered you're self up and approach the opponent with your devious smile carved across your radiant face. You get a cocktail and seated yourself across from the victim as a bait. He unexpectedly notice you and made eye contact with him. He glances at you once in a while and then back talking at his comrades.

"What are you waiting for go and make a move we're taking too much time here"

"Shut up jimin I can't focus if your always gonna chime in" you said in a whisper.

You waltz up towards him and seated at the empty space beside him. You looked with a seductive smirk rested on your face. "You look lonesome, want a company" you said in appealing tone. "Sure does, aren't you too young to like a old man like me" he said with a pint of sympathy in his words. "Not too old for me, let me get you a drink maybe a whisky?"

"Did you read my mind or something. that was quite impressive. Yes a whisky would be perfect"

You got a exclusive scoop about he's doleful lifestyle. He loves alcohol like his life is depending on it. it's like addicting drugs that keeps him alive and functioning. Without it he'd be doomed. Other than that there's nothing more he seem to care about rather than his beloved alcohol obsession.

"I'll be back wait for me will you" you head towards the bar and glanced around for any people near you. You swiftly get the micro bottle underneath your dress at the side of your thigh and vaguely spiked the alcohol and wait for the potion to dissolve. You put a grin on your face and head back to where he is.

"Did you miss me while I'm gone?"

"Not gonna lie I do miss the view of yours"

"Here's your Manhattan whisky laced with lime, cheers" you toast with him. "How did you know that this is what i usually go for?" As he take a sip of the alcohol laced with potion."Simple, I Did a little research about you and I found that you're the number one most powerful mafia boss. Too bad because in the matter of seconds you'll be out of that list" you give him a mischievous smirk.

His eyes widen in utter shock. Not being able to protest because of the fatal poison slowly encrypting to his entire body. His mouth becomes numb and his body started to go against his mind. "Don't fear I'm not going to kill you, I just want you to forget that you met this lady in a magenta dress" The chemical that you snuck in his drink can cause temporary amnesia of that previous memory he stored in his brain.

"So yeon tell Hoseok to meet me in the private lounge upstairs and prepared a escape plan just in case" jimin hurriedly said. the man suddenly collapsed on the floor earning a lot of attention from the guests near his location. You already escaped the scene instantly. You stared at his almost lifeless body laying qualmish on the hard floor. You avert your eyes distant away from that scene. You take a deep breath and retort back.

"I'll be on it" you immediately told Hoseok and get yourself out from that tableau you created.

Jimin ordered her to breakthrough a escape plan while him and Hoseok infiltrate the system and get through the body guards and hacked the locks in the designated metal passage. They are able to heist the golden Micro chip where the list of felonious deeds, confidential illegal acts and tons of forlorn casualty's of the competing gang will finally be exposed to the world and the people who been nothing but loyal them will no longer.

"So yeon where are you?" Hosoek quietly spoke to the earpiece

"I'm in the balcony of the mansion, it's clear you can walk to the corridors just don't make a noise people are still in the areas and I already took care of the cameras, you better hurry the security of the mansion are coming"

"Copy that, wait do you mean we're jumping down a eight storey building? Can you find another way"

"Are you being serious right now Hoseok"

"Okay fine I'll do it, just don't call me my first name again. I doesn't suit your pretty mouth"

"Then get over here fastly we're ruining out of time. Namjoon is going to pick us up at the corner alley"

You saw two black figures coming closer to your direction. You rapidly hid yourself at the back of the massive marble columns and grip your gun firmly in your fingers. Getting yourself ready in action. You peek at the incoming opponent and saw that the shadow is oddly shorter than the other one. You decided to make a move before they take can you down.

"Drop your weapons and put your hands up behind your head. don't move, I'm not hesitating to shoot" you shocked them as you saw them flinch.

"Chill So yeon we're not enemy's what ar-"

You cut his words. "How do you know my name and who the hell are you"

"This is complete nonsense let's just go" The guy on his left eagerly said.

"Don't you dare move" you pointed your gun at them trying to intimidate them.

"Let's stop this play seokjin's gonna be mad if we didn't make it to dinner" the man at the right uttered back.

"How do you kno-" they move their selves into the light making their face clear from the darkness that's been veil around them since they arrived. You took a deep sigh and loosen the grip of your pistol when you decipher that their not a threat perhaps they are your partners assign with you in this mission.

"I didn't mean to point a gun on both of you. I thought you were hostile"

"You thought wrong, plus I'm not petrified maybe jimin does" he uttered while tying the rope tightly to the marble columns.

"I'm not, just so you know" jimin defending himself. "Whatever you say, big boy" you said teasingly and throw him the last rope. "Are you ready?" The high heels were being remove at the moment. You didn't care of what their respond is gonna be you just glance at them once and jump to the fall of darkness.

You grab a hold of your halyard and use you feet to slowly go down at the side of the building. Both of them jump down and catch up to your fast pace skills despite of you wearing a skimpy gown in the cold dark night. You all reach the bottom part where you encounter the tall black figures. There's a massive green bushes enough to hide the three of you. You crouch down gripping your stilettos firmly in your hands as jimin and Hoseok entailed your movements carefully trying not to make a single sound. You looked back glaring intensely at them when suddenly a foot laid abruptly in your expensive dress not that it matters but you might trip and fall that will eventually ruin the whole mission. You saw them both nodded with their hands clasped together as they speak in a soft whisper apologising to what they've done not really knowing who did it in the first place. You successfully sneak past through the guards that's not paying attention to your smooth getaway. You sighted a black sports car and got inside and we escaped in tranquil.

Chapter 25

You took off your black stilettos and throw them across the room that's been a burden to your feet from doing those kinds of outlandish stunts that you're undertaking earlier. Fortunately you're accustomed to that stuff being the only girl in Namjoon's gang. You unfortunately have to look somewhat presentable at all cost. You enclosed the door and be blinded by the darkness around you but before you can speak to command the lights on. Someone pulled you to the mere corner. You saw his glistening eyes that seeming to glow in the dim lighting staring vastly at yours. He leans forward as your lips got contact with his but not enough to called it a kiss. You turn your head to avoid it. You distinguish instantaneously that he wasn't the man you've expected it to be. You touched his chest and gently pushed him centimeters away from you.

"What are you forbidding to do taehyung"

"Pardon me, I just missed your presence. I'm not practiced not seeing you all day"

"So you've awaited for me in my bedroom all morning until dawn is that what you're saying?" He nods in response. "Don't do that again if namjoon or any of them saw you or us together like this one of us is gonna get terminated you know he's rules taehyung. He breathes no mercy" you lied to him to make him back away. "Is he the reason, I'm talking about jungkook. Why is always got to be him" he pulled away from me and walked towards the door and glanced at me one more last before leaving. You saw the anguish and envious in his watery eyes as he left you feeling all kinds of emotion at once you couldn't decipher what exactly do you felt about this man. Emphatic and somber thats how you feel towards him.

When he saw him got out of her room he hesitated but he convinced himself not to get bothered by it and continue what he came for. He knocks on your door as he realize it was open. He saw you standing in front of him wearing this vampish magenta dress making his eyes dart away from glimpsing at your unflawed body.

"He liked you a lot, you know who I'm taking about the man that just got out of this room" I stared at him disagreeing to his words that slipped out his mouth. "I apologize for my actions the other day. There's no other way to redeem what I've done. I just lose myself when I'm faced with you, you make me weak. Life doesn't want me to be happy, to be with the person I love that's how cruel it is. But I couldn't live if the person who I truly love despise me. Forgive me and I will stay away from you as long as I can" he said with all sincerity. You slowly turn your body around. Him back facing you as you speak what's been bothering your mind in the last few days. "How can I not forgive the man that I love. That's like hurting your own self. Avoiding him is the most challenging mission I have to endure. Loving the person you can't have is tormenting"

"Can you speak that again I think I heard it wrong. Do you really felt the same way about me or I'm just hallucinating"

"I wasn't finding for love but when I found you it changes my perception of what you called love is. It's not exactly how I paint it out in my head but at the end it's you jungkook you got me, you finally won"

You turned your body to his direction. He bend down to your face as his eyes dart from your eyes trailing down to what he labeled the red cherry lips of yours. You remembered how it make your heart jump just by his bare touch and satisfying words that always kept you on edge. But you force yourself not to fall for it but in this case scenario it's otherwise. You have fallen vastly in to him. His minty breath fans over your lips and he stared at your perfect features. Not waiting any longer he pressed his lips against yours. His lips were sweet and passionate not like the previous one. Your hands wraps around his neck and his hands traced the gentle curves of your body. Things are heating up by the second. Once his hands get a hold of the zipper of your dress you knew that your obligated to stop before it could go any further oppose to what your body want and what you've been longing. As you pushed his chest gently.

"I understand...I know you're not ready, I'll leave and give you space to yourself" You nod not wanting to explain what's inside your mind and whats it begging to protest. "No please don't leave me can you stay beside me until morning" he smiled and intertwined his hands to yours as he brings me to the bed and we both sat down. "Jungkook if you mind I need to get dressed properly"

"Sure, I'll be waiting out here if that's okay with you" he uttered shyly "it's fine, wait for me" You got of the bathroom wearing your proper attire to sleep in. You glimpse at him laying on the bed in serenity. You slid underneath the silky white sheets and enfold your arms around his waist and rested your head in his firm chest. You felt his heart beating as fast as he make yours every time you're in his presence. He pulled you even closer to him as you met his gaze. The scene in your head that you've been dreaming about the perfect scenario you've always dying to know what it feels like. Being comfortable in complete silence. Being next to the person you adore and cared about. Finally it's enfolding right before your very eyes. "Jungkook can you tell me a story perhaps something about you"

"Okay but if you tell me yours after mine"

"I thought you already knew, you're not that obsessed at me as I thought you would"

"I know a few details, never mind I'm going to continue my enlightening story"

There was boy who always wanted one thing but his parents lack in it. So he tried anything he can to prove himself that he's deserving of that one thing but they did it seem to acknowledge his hardships and sacrifices so he ran away from them, from home.

Away from what he called family and found a new one where he could get this thing he's been wanting all his life. Love. he didn't find them but instead they find him and took care of him noting like his parents could ever give.

He felt happiness once. not until he met this wonderful girl that changed his life drastically he loved this woman with all of his heart and will never want to change that even if they don't last together or she found someone else He will always be here right beside her.

"That was mind opening really, but it's doesn't feel right to abandon your parents just like that, I grew up without a single one of them. It's didn't felt great at all it's almost self wrenching but I need to survive to fulfill my fathers last words to find my brother. That's why I'm here In this position just being a puppet to him but I owed namjoon a lot. he's the one who helped me out of my misery I applaud him for that I'm more than thankful that I met them, my saviors"

"We have a lot of similarity's I also grew with my gang there the ones who stand as my parents and I owe them everything that I am right now, they who I've become they made me" He sit up from the bed as you follows his movements imitating what he does. He rested his hands on top of mine and brushed the hair strands away from my face as he tucked it behind my ears and smile softly at me but his grin fades faintly making me frown my eye brows from the sudden change of expression he's displaying right in front of you. "So yeon you know that it's impossible for us to keep this hidden forever right?" he suddenly asked you this question you've been avoiding. "I'm aware, let's date in secret then" You desperately caressed his cheeks as he touched your fingers that softly laying at the side of his face.

"Now? it's just not...now" you vigorously shook your head at his response "Why not?...tell me jungkook"

"Their watching my every move. They already gave me a warning and I don't want you to be involved in this mess. We can't be... together not now" he sadly mumbled the very last words. You're eyes widen in disbelief. You couldn't believe what's coming out of his lips. After everything you just professed to him. He's just gonna throw away your feelings like it's nothing. You felt your heart sunk down to the pit of your stomach. As you pictured him leaving your side forever. You convince yourself that you need to affray and protest not letting another person left you once again even if it takes you to be vulnerable and put down your guards. You'll do anything for the person you're devoted with. "Don't be like that jungkook, we'll make it work somehow. We will fight for as long as we have each other" He faintly smiled in reassurance as he pulled you into a embrace as you felt him fall asleep in your warm company. You stared at his now sleeping figure. His parted lips, his perfect nose and the way he breath is just...

He's really is beautiful...

You made me bestowed everything entailing my own self and I know boundless inside that it's all worth it. I hope this is not just an infatuation that trick us that we are devoted to the other person perhaps fake love, but instead the real love that we've been hunting all our existence. You behold this blissful feeling,

It's Love....

We need each other the most, you won't be able to love without your other half...without me.

Milton Keynes UK
Ingram Content Group UK Ltd.
UKHW022024131124
451149UK00013B/1292